❧ Aunt Pig of Puglia ❧

Ricordi de la Familia Ferri

Patricia Catto

PATRICIA CATTO

❧ Aunt Pig of Puglia ❧
Ricordi de la Familia Ferri

Patricia Catto

Jaded Ibis Press
an imprint of Jaded Ibis Productions, Inc.
Kansas City, Missouri U.S.A.

PATRICIA CATTO

COPYRIGHTED MATERIAL

Cover design and illustrations by Debra Di Blasi.
Fine art limited edition book, signed archival prints of illustrations, and full color "Tarocco del Porco" ("Tarot of the Pig" cards) are available at http://jadedibisproductions.com

❧ TABLE OF CONTENTS ❧

Author's Note

The Latin spelling of "family" in the *Aunt Pig of Puglia* subtitle ("familia" rather than Italian "famiglia") is intentional, referring to the clan-like social structure that was essentially designed to reflect the ancient Roman state. But, as you shall see, my family was an example not of *pater* familia but of *mater* familia!

❧ Pasquale's Preface ❧

My given name at birth was Patrizia, a nice noble name, and one for a female – a gender I still claim. But that name didn't want me. My father, from the time I was three, called me "Pasquale," which as you may know is a boy's name. Why he called me Pasquale was not something he himself knew. I didn't resemble any Pasquales in his life or anything of the sort. The name, he explained, had chosen me and used him as its conduit. The proof? It stuck to me like glue.

Names, he believed, are willful like that – and so are stories. They choose who they want to carry them into the world – and push the people they choose around, leaving them little say in the whole matter. (Stories, see, were here before we were.)

One reason I must write the stories of my people, the ones you are about to read, is that the stories themselves demand it. Believe me when I tell you, I am somewhat lazy by nature and would not have gone to the elaborate lengths it takes to write all these things down, had I not from early days been compelled to do.

They often ask more than I'm capable of doing, really. For if they could, they'd paint you every bristle on Aunt Pig's spine, every freckle on Aunt Ciara's face. They're like that, with their lust for detail. But, hey, they do know there's only so much they can expect of me, and then I have to let you, beloved reader, do the rest. (They know where you live, too.)

9

Another reason I'm telling you these stories is that it will piss off my mother to the end of forever. And that is something that, as you'll discover, our relationship demands. That's how my mother keeps our family ties strong — through unceasing squabbling, rampant projection, and ignorant miscommunication. Our identities absolutely count on such.

Now, if after reading this last bit of information, you begin to ask, "Who the hell are these people and what kind of a crazy, preposterous family am I getting in this book?"

Well, that's just the question you should be asking.

Continue, dear reader. We're a good pair already. Keep going, turn the page. *Benvenuto, grazie!*

Andiamo!

il passato

❧ Aunt Pig ❧

In which my Great Aunt Ada is born with bristles and other controversial features

"We come," my mother explained early, "from a long line of pigs."

Actually, it's one particular pig, the Pig Aunt, of whom she spoke. (But over-dramatization, you'll soon see, is a trick of which my people, my mother included, never tire.)

The Pig Aunt was born in *our* village in Casamassima, in the province of Bari. This is also known as Apulia, the region famous for tasty fish dishes and Moorish flavorings and *i trulli* – conical-shaped ovens.

The Pig Aunt then is indeed locatable outside myth, kind of on the boot heel of Italy, on the Adriatic Sea in the little Casamassima village on Garibaldi Street. And she came into the world in the normal way, not Cesarean or anything – which I guess is more a Roman birth method, isn't it?

I'm joking already, digressing.

Anyway, her name was Ada Posa and she had, at birth, boar bristles running up and down her infant spine. And she looked more four footed, more like a little pig with pink trotters than a human girl with hands, toes, etc.

Everyone was upset. Santo Rocco is the patron saint of Casamassima and has a sidekick that is a little dog, sort of a spiritual form of Buster Brown and Tige.

The women there pray to Saint Rocco first, then to the Virgin. When, however, they saw Ada emerge into the world, some went all the way to God. That is to say they behaved like Protestants.

It was not expected, this kind of a baby. One with six toes, maybe. But this – Jesus!

A lot of people knew great-aunt Ada's mother had probably sinned to get this kind of baby. She'd probably considered abortion, since it was her eleventh pregnancy, and this was the payback. God sent a pig to give her a clue about right thinking.

Or maybe it was because she was so good, the other theory went. She got the pig because God knew she could take anything he gave her. And keep smiling. Boils, scrofula – just like Job, the luckiest of mortals: sometimes being cursed meant you were in favor – in REVERSE.

Suffering, see, it's really about being LUCKY!

Who really knew, God being so unfathomable. That's finally what people said to great-aunt Ada's mother when they wanted to be politically correct.

"Who knows what God had in mind," they'd say, "up His sleeve, on the back burner of grace..."

Quite obviously, though, it was a pig.

Great-aunt Ada was given a half-crib, half-manger type sleeping arrangement. And everyone wanted to see her, roiling limply there in the straw. Some were a little hesitant, but curiosity won over good manners, introversion, and everything else.

The village beat a path to little Ada's door. Just as if there were a dark star shining over her manger, if you catch my comparison.

They all went to see her under the flimsy pretext of comforting her family, meanwhile pirouetting with the lust for sensation and the delicious misfortune of SOMEONE ELSE.

Of course, this kind of madcap fun couldn't last.

The Pig Aunt died after only fourteen years. But all the while she was alive, people came from all over Apulia – and farther – to gawk at her.

"To the credit of your good family," my mother pointed out, "no admission charge was ever considered. Not even for a minute!"

My mother would cluck and go, "*Peccata, Peccata!* Poor Thing! Poor Thing!" when she'd describe Aunt Pig's wake.

"She was covered up in a white, embroidered sheet – ironed just beautiful, starched nice, with just her shriveled little snout protruding. Oh God, she suffered the pains of hell, that poor Pig.

"And they made her a little cap because she was still like a child in size. A little white lace cap. Can't you just see how pitiful it looked on her grey head? Oh God. So pathetic. No real hair, just a thick strand here and there – bristles – very sparse on her skull. Oh, God.

"And muscles? No way. She'd never been able to stand up or walk. Oh God, I don't want to talk about it. Please God, take her sufferings from my mind. Sweet innocent pig. Why do we suffer so in this life? Why? I better shut up before God sends me worse. Who am I to question Him?"

And, as she'd describe the scene, my mother would close her eyes and for good measure cover them with her hands, trying to banish Aunt Pig.

"Oh God," I'd say too, even as a child. "I wish I could've helped her. I'd have picked her up and put her in a carriage and shown her stuff. I'd have LOVED her."

"No, are you crazy?" my mother'd say, all disgusted. "She had to stay on her side; her bones were brittle. No one could pick her up. She suffered the PAINS OF HELL!"

It was so disconcerting, Aunt Pig's plight. But even worse, my mother always capped the story off with the real kicker.

"You've got the pig genes in your family, little girl. You see how hairy we all are? Cousin Tanny has a beard even now. Doesn't shave, though I think it's disgraceful. Actually, it might grow in thicker if she did, but she should do something. Uh...um... It runs in the family is the point. So don't feel too smart about your looks. We're not out of the woods with this pig business yet. A pig could show up again."

il formaggio

❧ Après Aunt Pig, Le Deluge ❧

In which Casamassima flounders in the grip of an identity crisis

Though only a child at the time, my mother, when pressed, remembered what took place after the somewhat untimely demise of Aunt Pig. Unprepared for normalcy, Casamassima plunged into a slough of despondency from which it had a hard time recovering.

Without Aunt Pig, the town had lost its raison d'être, its calling card, its claim to fame. And from all accounts, it blamed Aunt Pig's family, the Posa's. Somehow it was their fault that Aunt Pig was no longer around or that she'd been there and suddenly left them in the lurch. To them it was like the Doges in Venice had filled up the canals and then skipped off to Switzerland for a vacation.

"That's people for you," scoffed my mother. "Did they care about Aunt Pig or our family in any real way? No! No way. They acted like Sicilians, all of them. Do you know what they wanted to do to her, your poor great-aunt after she died?"

"What, Mama?"

"Stuff her, that's what!"

"No," called my father from upstairs where he was resting. "It wouldn't have been *stuffing* her at all! It would have been mummification."

"Stuffing is what it would've amounted to," insisted my mother growing irate over the memory as well as my father's editorial. "Stuffing is a Sicilian deal. They

15

have whole caves and churches with stuffed people in them – from back in the old, old times. They love that stuffing technique and the people in Casamassima wanted to do it to Aunt Pig, God rest her, and put her on display forever!"

"Maybe she would have looked really nice?" I ventured.

"What? Do you have any human blood in your veins? If you died would you want me to stuff you and prop you up in the middle of the Piazza – forget it – it's sick – the people here were sick – are you going to stuff *me* when *I* die, Pasquale?"

"So what happened?" I asked, all chastised and cowed.

"Nothing happened. Aunt Pig's mother buried her like a decent mother. Then the next thing was they tried to poke around and maybe see if Aunt Pig had done any miracles or anything, see if they could get her nominated to sainthood and get a little fame off her that way."

"So did they?"

"No, are you nuts? What miracles could Aunt Pig have done? She could hardly blink her eyes or grunt, poor wasted soul. She couldn't speak or pray or any of it. And they'd never been sure if she even understood what was told her!"

"So what did they do then?"

"Oh, just ridiculous stuff. They'd remembered once holding a picture of San Gennaro up to her and she had breathed on it or something."

"Well, was that good?"

"Oh yeah," said my mother sarcastically. "That was great. A miracle, for sure. Somebody though had remembered that bit of fluff and tried to build it up. But they didn't get far. Aunt Pig was just not saint material. The Bishop finally wrote a letter and told Casamassima that he didn't even know what species Aunt Pig was and that they were lucky she'd even had the sacraments, let alone be considered for sainthood."

"That Bishop sounds rather mean, Mama, rather cold."

"No, he was fed up is all, fed up with human greed and stupidity. Aunt Pig's mother wrote back and thanked him on behalf of our whole family – for letting things get back to normal.

"But that didn't work either. Once there's been a famous pig or something like that in a community or a family, no one forgets too easily. And normal becomes a dream you just can't reach anymore. Everything goes haywire. I suppose you don't remember hearing about your Great-Aunt Lena Posa, do you, Pasquale? She got the worst of this whole deal!"

"No, I do remember. She's the one who became the atheist lawyer in Brazil, right? The sister Grandma Ferri never saw again."

"Jesus, you don't forget much do you? Yeah, well little Lena was the one who was hit hardest by having a sister who was a pig. Why am I telling you all this anyway? If you could, you'd just have me tell you tales all damn day. What a waste of breath! Anyway, Lena got stuck as a kid watching people fuss over Ada and then seeing them fighting over the sainthood business and it twisted her up. She just didn't know what was quite real anymore or who to believe in. So in the end, she gave up God and became a lawyer in Brazil. That's right. That's how that went."

"But how exactly did it happen, Mama? How did she just give up God and suddenly she's in Brazil all educated and a lawyer? How do things like that happen?"

17

"Hey, Pasquale, you're asking the wrong person. I only know she started off religious enough, just like the rest of us — more so maybe, always studying church rules and the kinds of sins and levels of angels and all that. She reminds me of you, actually — all that nit-pick work — and then, something turned her the other way..."

❧ Great-Aunt Lena's Confession ❧

In which Father Nuzzi teaches about perfect acts of contrition and the resultant confusion

"Bless me, Father, for I have sinned. My last confession was two weeks ago and these are my sins."

"Go ahead, my child," said Father Nuzzi to Great-Aunt Lena Posa, who was a twisted knot of girlish misery.

"Well, I'm not perfectly sure what I did is a sin, uh…"

"Hey, I'll figure it out. Go ahead and tell me. If it's a sin, I'll spot it. Go ahead, child."

"Well, I prayed my sister would die and she did. Is that a sin?"

"Hmmmm. Probably. Yes. But tell me the circumstances. Wait, do I know your sister?"

"Yes, Father. My sister was Ada Posa."

"The PIG?"

"Yes, the now deceased Pig."

"Ohhhh. I see."

"Yes, Father. I prayed she'd die and she did."

"Well, now listen, my child. For you to humbly ask that God end her suffering would not be wrong. Were you thinking of your dear sister's welfare in that prayer?"

"Oh, no. I was thinking of how convenient it would be to have the little room off the kitchen free of her –

and also that she was getting, rather, you know – oh, not too fragrant."

"My child! That unfortunate soul was hardly responsible for her condition. God sent her that affliction and you as her sister were there to ease her, not judge her or point out her odors."

"So it's a sin what I did?"

"Yes. I feel that it is. I feel you should ask God to forgive it right now."

"Well, that's the idea in coming. But there's a problem."

"What? What problem?"

"It occurred to me that if my mother should have another one like Ada – you know, a second pig – I'd pray the same. So I'm not sorry enough, I guess. But I am afraid of being excommunicated *and* damned!"

"Now, you're just a little girl! It's young Lena, isn't it? Why so fearful of such things? Why not search your heart and realize you're very, very sorry for questioning God's will and wanting Him to take your sister away just so you could have more room?"

"I can't lie to Him on top of it, Father. I wanted her gone so much. I couldn't even look at her. You saw her – all grey and wheezy. You didn't like her, did you? You sort of stood as far away as possible when you gave her extreme unction, remember? Remember you had your handkerchief over your nose?"

"No. I remember nothing of the kind. Anyway, Lena, it's you we're worrying about. Do you want to confess or not?"

"That's what I'm saying. I can't make a perfect confession over a bad sin – so I'm damned. I'm damned to hellfire, right? If I die tonight I'm going down, not up. And you can't help me because you can't change my heart. That's the rules."

"I can only tell you to pray to God until you *are* sorry. Then come back."

"But what if I get killed later on today? Isn't there anything you can tell me to help me? What if there's an earthquake soon? Can't you help?"

"But I can't really. No. I can pray *for* you, Lena, that God softens your attitude and opens up your heart."

"Father! It's not fair. Ada got all the attention when she was alive and *she* never had to clean up after me. *I* always had to take care of *her*. All she did was lie around and look like an animal and everybody LOVED it! It made me sick. It did! And now because of her I'm going to *hell*. I'm going to HELL! At the worst, she's got a month in Purgatory. But I'm going to *HELL!*"

At this prospect, Lena left the confessional, exasperated. She looked around at the interior of a church she no longer felt could save her. She couldn't even go to Holy Communion anymore because she couldn't go to Confession.

She decided to try and talk to Jesus honestly, just a little. She genuflected, rose, crossed herself and moved to the center of a pew near the altar where a large crucifix hung.

"You are the enthroned Son of God. And I am just the unloved sister of a deceased pig. You came to save everyone but now I don't believe you can save me. I feel low and so guilty – but not truly sorrowful and repentant. Can you help me? Send me a sign."

Nothing happened to reassure Lena that she was heard. So she continued.

"Look, Father Nuzzi didn't really even like Ada. Isn't it obvious to You he was lying about the handkerchief over his nose? I saw the whole, nauseated way he acted with Ada – and so did You. I believe in You, You know I do. Can't You help me? Please! Please!

"Just give me some little sign. Show me You know I did my best to try and love Ada. Is it my fault I couldn't? She was a sickening sort, Lord Jesus!

"I mean honestly, isn't it just possible when You were in human form that You might've had a hard time with Ada? With all her physical problems? Just a little hint of disgust? Maybe?"

No response. No sign.

"Actually," Lena said as she rose to leave, "I just remembered that you were really good with the lepers. So never mind. I'm just too flawed to bother with right now. As usual, Ada's the lucky one in the family. It's not like she ever has to worry. I guess Paradise was made just for pigs like her? Maybe I'm feeling a little bit glad for her here? Is that maybe a sign of some kind? God, I hope so!

"But, wait! Is there possibly, *maybe* something I could read in Saint Augustine, a case like mine which might give me some pointers on how to handle this? Any precedents? Anything documented?

"Am I talking to myself here?"

❧ The Death Sisters ❧

In which the Posa Sisters and their suspicious widowhoods are recalled

My mother didn't much go for her cousins, the Death Sisters.

The only difference between crows and the Death Sisters, she'd say with a sneer, is that crows had better singing voices, better legs, and didn't wear white lipstick!

Crows, you know how they are, eat what's dead and mashed up a little. And they find such fare nourishing, *delizioso*.

The saying in Italian for when you have a good appetite is *buona forchetta*: "You have a good fork."

And the good fork the Death Sisters had was for sticking in permanently ill, dying, or dead people. They went to great lengths to be near such individuals, and I might tell you (no surprises, I'm sure), that it was Anna Posa, head Death Sister, who crocheted Aunt Pig's burial cap. And a fine and painstaking job she did.

The Death Sisters were Fiora, Anna, and Maria. They had a house all to themselves a couple blocks away from my grandparents' home.

Casamassima, a very small village at that time you see, was designed with nosy people in mind. The Death Sisters, from their vantage point at the crest of a little hill, could see not only the church and the undertaker's from their upstairs bedrooms, but also my grandparents' home and many, many other relatives' dwellings.

il morte

And that suited them just fine. If anyone had so much as an inflamed toenail, they were sure to draw a bead on it and begin watching closely.... just in case.

The Death Sisters had not always lived in their nicely situated crow's nest. At one time they'd all been married to their respective husbands and had lived with them. But one by one (through careful planning perhaps) the Death Sisters' husbands had departed. My father's belief was that they'd died in self-defense. But then he was such a cynic.

Fiora's husband had died mad. For some reason he had taken to sweeping everything in (and out) of sight, tidying up with a vengeance. Fiora didn't mind so much except for the night he crawled out onto their roof and swept snow off it – all night. And even though it was hot summer and there wasn't any snow, not any, he died of a bad chill. The raw power of the mind amazed everyone.

At that time, Fiora, Anna and Maria found their true calling in life. So many flowers, hams, cakes and sympathy cards passed into Fiora's well-swept home that the sisters took notice. A bloom came upon them.

They all three began to wear deep, deep black, attend mass every day, take daily strolls to the mausoleum. They started to visit invalids without ceasing.

Fiora's loss was soon whetted when Maria's husband died within three months of his crazed brother-in-law. He was walking by a tavern when a chair flew out of it and brained him. (The chair had been involved in a brawl, which is why it behaved with such volition, trying to escape the uncouth men who were worrying it so.)

With Maria's husband dead so soon on the heels of Fiora's dear spouse, all eyes fell on Anna. Or more specifically, on her husband.

By no means insensitive to the trend he saw developing, Anna's husband left her for another woman. But that stuff never works. If this man had read *Oedipus* or some equally powerful classic that explains Fate's stranglehold on us, he'd have just killed himself and saved time and energy. But he wasn't a reader.

Nevertheless, for a while things looked promising for him. His new girlfriend was termed That Dirty Bag by the Death sisters, my mother and her own sisters, their mother, her mother-in-law, and all other decent women who had to wait for their men to die in order to be done with them. So you know That Dirty Bag was really good looking and was making Anna's husband happy.

He dropped by to see Anna now and again to bring her fresh vegetables and cry about how torn his heart felt, but that he was too afraid to return to her. He wept and gave squash to her, just enough so that she felt he might come back permanently. But that was wishful thinking on Anna's part.

He bought That Dirty Bag a house, developed a bone disease, and died in her arms.

The Death Sisters heard about it, of course, and went right to the lawyer. Before he was cold, Anna wanted the right to lay her husband out, arrange his funeral, and get That Dirty Bag's house. Also, she wanted That Dirty Bag to realize that wearing black was a wife's prerogative.

But That Dirty Bag was plucky. She laid out Anna's husband in their home, got her own family to man the door, and threw out the wreath which came from the florist – the huge rose and carnation wreath which spelled out Beloved Husband.

Not to be outdone, the Death Sisters fished the wreath out of the trash where it was not resting in peace and marched it to the front door. They demanded that Anna be allowed to pay her respects to her husband.

That Dirty Bag came to the door and told the Sisters that they were dried up prunes, old ghouls, and had flat asses. She further pointed out that Anna was soon to be homeless because Cesare (yes, Anna's husband had a name) loved That Dirty Bag and had willed her Anna's house as well as the love nest in which they'd so recently flourished.

In addition to the shameless abuse she heaped on the Sisters, she did it from inside a tight, sheath dress of richest, velvety black, the kind of black experienced only near the River Styx and its environs. It screamed tragic, sex widow of Milanese haute couture majesty of the centuries.

And for that dress alone, The Death Sisters vowed eternal warfare on That Dirty Bag.

Not quite sure how to deal with That Dirty Bag, and with the opportunity of Cesare's spectacular funeral hanging like a carrot before them, the Death Sisters repaired themselves to my mother's house. They needed witnesses to their tragedy and maybe some advice on how to make That Dirty Bag heel.

My mother saw the three trooping up the street and surmised the situation. She went back to the kitchen, slammed down the focaccia dough with malice, wiped her hands and said, "Here come these bitches, right in the middle of my work day. They'll never leave now. They give me the creeps."

As soon as they crossed the threshold though, it was a different story.

"Oh, oh, Anna. I feel so sick that *you* had to come to see *me*. And at such a time. Oh, we were coming over to see you tonight. Oh, God. Sit down, cousins. Have some anisette. Oh, God. Anna. What's going on with That Dirty Bag? She's a scourge, and now especially..."

Well, the Death Sisters spilled the whole tale, complete with legal complications and the grim possibility of being shut out of Cesare's funeral. It took a long time. They began in medias res and kept going back and forth in time.

It was a great and memorable Kitchen scene. Three women in black interviewing another woman sur-

rounded by flour clouds, aproned, and visibly per-
turbed by something big, archetypal.

I looked at my mother's face and saw:

Nothing was ever supposed to interfere with daily
work routines.

Nothing.

And the Death Sisters were transgressing, *liberally*,
full of themselves and oblivious to their precarious
position. They took my mother's suffocated rage as
proof of her loyalty to their cause. They were
encouraged by it.

Their white lips like six, slivery fishes kept moving
in the gloom of the kitchen. Finally, they got up to
leave, eloquent with hopelessness, holding to one
another.

My mother, too, rose to the occasion. And she gave
them the gift they needed. When all was said and done,
she came through for them, showing once again what
family was all about; she lied through her teeth.

"Cousins, you are in a war here, a war which
demands the most delicate strategy to win. There is
only one way to assure victory.

"You must dress up and go to your dear husband's
funeral and sit in front of the church. It's your right. If
he didn't love you, he'd have divorced you. Everybody
knows he didn't really love That Dirty Bag.

"She got him to sign the house over when he was
delirious, a weak moment. Bone disease makes people
do funny things. He used to bring you fresh squash, so
it shows who he cared about, right? His heart never
moved from your side. I know. I was at your wedding
and I remember how he looked at you. You were *it!*

"So just dress up, you and your sisters, and go right
to the front of the church. And if That Dirty Bag

comes in and makes a fuss, just move a little out of the way and let her act like the stray bitch she is.

"Everyone knows she's just clinging to straws and you are the wife. They'll side with you. They know the tragedies you and Fiora and Maria have endured. They know you're saints. Cousins, you are the saints of this town – stainless, pure, self-sacrificing. Everyone is indebted to you and loves you.

"It'll all come out. You'll see. Go. Claim your right. Cesare's still your husband. And listen, just to be one step ahead of you-know-who, go order his mausoleum spot right now. And get one for you right above him! Have both your names on it – know what I mean?"

Oh, how the Death Sisters loved this last shrewd suggestion. They kissed my mother's floury fingers a hundred times (something she hated, of course) and hugged her, now crying more with gratitude than grief.

On her way down to the street, Fiora called back to my mother, "Palma, we knew to come and see you for help. You *think* like us. You are our general. Oh, God bless you, Palma. *Cugina. Grazie, mille grazie.*"

My mother shut the door and shook her head. "Bitches! I'm so behind now, I'll never catch up. A completely wasted day."

My father, the coast clear, came downstairs equally disgusted. "Are the crows going to go pick Cesare's diseased bones?"

"Hey," said my mother. "Don't start on those girls. They're my cousins. And don't bother to side with Cesare, either. He never gave two shits about Anna. Worthless man. Trash. God rest his soul. I shouldn't speak so of the dead."

"But you said he LOVED her," I reminded my mother, alarmed. "Didn't he LOVE her? You said he LOVED her."

29

"Of course he didn't love her," my mother shrieked. "He gave her house away to That Dirty Bag he took up with. Is that LOVE?"

"Well, why did you say to Anna how much he loved her? You lied to her, Mama. You were lying."

"No. I didn't lie to her. And besides, if I told the truth, she'd still be here crying and bothering me. So leave me alone. It's not my business to sort out who loves who. If you worry about LOVE and all that crap, you never get anything done. Love's for weak-minded people with nothing better to do."

"That's right," said my father, en route to his nap.

"Hey," my mother snapped, immediately worked up. "What do you know about love?"

❧What My Father Knew About Love ❧

In which my father relates the startling confession of his early marriage

Obviously, my father knew a lot about love. He knew he didn't have it. And he knew if he'd been so fortunate to get it, he'd have been the luckiest man alive.

But that wasn't going to be his story.

One day, with the most solemn exposition – a formal invitation he extended to me to go with him for coffee in the piazza – he discussed his shocking secret.

"Yes, Pasquale, it went like this. The morning after my wedding night, I woke to see your mother's face sleeping near me on the pillow. And a feeling of panic overtook me. I wanted to flee to the mountains or disappear or kill myself. I didn't know which.

"Your mother, she was really tired. She'd had to strangle all the chickens for our wedding banquet herself – strangle them and bake them up. Her sisters and your grandmother were busy doing everything else.

"And I looked at her and I could tell she was still mad, resentful at all the work she'd had to do the day before her wedding. You know your mother – all business, all work. But underneath – lazy. Lazy as can be. And with the belief deep within that she should be Queen.

"Every single day of her life she's mad at somebody because she's not Queen. And I saw it there on the pillow that first morning, saw that she'd be mad as a wet hen forever.

"Well, what to do about it? I couldn't give her what she desired, though in the beginning I tried. A curious thing happened just before we wed. My old sweetheart, Elena, told me to meet her behind the church; she had something to tell me.

"My instincts were against going to meet with her. I still liked her too much, you see. But I went. What a mistake. She told me not to marry your mother. She admitted being too hasty in breaking off our courtship earlier in the year. She spelled out every one of your mother's faults and left none unnoticed. Elena had known your mother for years, since girlhood, and she was an accurate judge of character.

"So she begged me to call off the wedding, knowing full well that your mother's temperament would kill my life.

"And you know, she was right.

"How awful to admit this to you, my only daughter. But it's true. And you must know how I feel.

"Your mother is a murderess – full of crazy contradictions, self-pity, false stoicism. And she has no imagination. She has no logic. No hope of tolerating another being's idiosyncrasies, no fluidity. No compassion for me whatsoever.

"And she's very provincial, very narrow.

"My people, Pasquale, and they're your people, too, are from the North. We're from Treviso and that has a certain weight to it around here. It's sad to say but Casamassima is so backwards compared to the North. There's just no comparing it. I'm in all ways a fish out of water here. Someday, you'll travel. You'll see. But for now, just trust me. It matters where you come from. You carry the earth on which you were born with you. Always."

My father paused dramatically.

"Yes, it's like with vampires," I volunteered. It was the first thing I'd said in an hour.

My father blinked, startled out of his soulful reverie and confession. "What vampires?"

"Well, they can travel, but they always have to have a coffin filled with their home soil to sleep in. Else they die."

My father looked at me incredulously. I could tell he was debating whether or not the gravity of the situation had sunk into me.

It was a little trick I had, pretending to be dense or literal-minded during particularly heavy, uncomfortable times. It was the defense I favored.

He looked at me critically. "But you understand what I've told you today?"

"Yes, I do."

"Well, good. Then you see why my depression is so deep. I told you today adult-to-adult about it. So honor this confidence, Pasquale. And choose wisely when you come to marry."

With that, my father had completed his mission. He put his tiny espresso cup down on the green marble top of the table with a little fateful clink and gazed off vacantly, heroically.

My own eyes wandered over the piazza, to the fountain in the center. Today there was a puppet show set up near it and I watched the puppets fussing and fighting from my seat. I'd seen them a million times over the years.

They were always having the same quarrels and preoccupations, these puppets. Usually I liked their energy and their tenacity. But right now they seemed somewhat menacing.

If it were possible for a man to look at his new bride's face on the pillow and love her no more, everything was changed.

My father, I could tell, did sort of understand my mother. She was as rough as a hurricane. And just as blameless.

But he couldn't love her, even though he understood this. The winds near her were just too strong. So what were they going to do about the situation?

My guess was nothing. Nothing was something people did frequently when confronted with overwhelming problems. And something does come of nothing, contrary to what King Lear says.

I, for instance, wasn't going to worry about being the child of divorce or abandonment. My parents' cage of inertia suited me and I walked around in it feeling secure, if not smug.

il matrimonio

❧ My Mother ❧

In which my mother relates the bloody details of her wedding feast and explains *Honore!*

As soon as we got home from our discussion, my father beat it upstairs to his room and I was left to my mother's suspicions.

"So. Where did you and your foolish father go all hush-hush?" she said, eyeing me like the Sphinx of Thebes, kind of hungry after not having eaten anyone for a while.

I invoked evasion-by-half-truth. "Oh, just to the piazza for coffee."

"Oh, is that right? So what earth-shattering discussions came up there, pray may I ask?"

"Well, he told me about what kinds of food you had at your wedding."

"What? Why? Who cares after this many years. It's digested by now, believe me! So what kind did he say we had?"

"Just baked chicken."

"Just baked chicken? Let me tell you, little girl, that it was not JUST baked chicken. It was chickens I knew very well. Thirty the most unfortunate creatures that ever died for no reason. To celebrate what, I'd like to know, those poor bastards. To celebrate the end of my happiness and the beginning of my life as a slave?

35

"Thirty of them I had to kill with my own hands. It was blood everywhere. Never again, I said. Never another one. I got absolutely no help from anyone. But your father's family all came and stuffed their faces, let me tell you. Northern barbarians.

"It was the beginning of the end. Only one human being saw the truth. And that was Nonno Catto, your father's father, God rest his soul. He plunked down beside me at the bridal table, put his head down on it, and cried.

"He'd cry and look up at me every once in awhile. And then he'd take my hands and look in my eyes and cry. He said, 'Palma, you poor girl-so-good. You don't deserve this. Marrying my William. Oh, poor girl.'

"It struck me as pretty strange, of course. Him crying like that. But what did I know, foolish innocent that I was?

"Well, about two weeks after the wedding, it started. A bill collector came to the house and asked me for money. Do you know for what?"

"The chickens?"

"No, ridiculous girl. Not the chickens. They were our chickens. Grandpa Ferri's chickens."

"Oh."

"My wedding ring!"

"What?"

"Yes, your father had charged my wedding ring to me. Do you know how that made me feel?"

"Bad. Very horrible."

"Yes, I'd say a little worse than bad. Are you kidding? And then, it really began. Your father would go to work in the morning and by noon, he'd come home sick, complaining, bellyaching. This hurt or that hurt or something else was twinging around in him or

– Oh! – who can keep up with all that was going wrong with him? I can't.

"To make a long story short, he never worked a full day in his life after we got married – as if you haven't noticed."

"But he's sick."

"No, he's not sick. He's the Rajah of Punjab. And I manage his spa! I'm the sick one because I work day in and day out to take care of us all – and he naps!"

"But he's depressed. His heart's been broken. You always said he was sick and we needed to care for him."

"Well, I said that to you when you were a child so you wouldn't be too ashamed of him. But if you want the truth, he's a lazy hypochondriac and he knows a good thing when he sees it. He knows my focaccia and my noodles have made us a fortune. They're famous all over the world."

"All over the world?"

"You know what I mean. I mean everybody eats them. I know what I'm doing."

"But why have you stayed with him all these years if he's so bad?"

"Why? Because he's my husband. Do you think I want people to laugh at me and make fun of you for having a no-good father?"

"I guess it would be okay."

"WHAAATT? Is that what you're going to stand there and say, you ingrate? Oh, you're impossible...."

"Well, if you hate him and you're miserable...I'm only thinking of you!"

"Who said I hate him? He's a very smart man, your father. He's lazy, but he's also very smart. His family's all very smart too. They're writers and opera singers and that one went over to India and studied their religion or whatever. They're highly cultured."

"But you don't live with them. You live with him. And you said he's lazy and – "

"Hey, lower your voice. You want him to hear? One thing I have and you don't is family loyalty!"

"Why don't I have family loyalty? Who said I don't?"

"Talking about your father like I should get rid of him. Is that very loyal?"

"But you're the one who was telling his faults! Telling me he takes advantage of you!"

"What faults? So what? Everybody's got faults. If you got rid of somebody just because they had faults, there'd be no more marriages."

"Yeah, well what if you found out you were like Anna Posa and Papa was like Cesare and he didn't love you?"

"Your father? Not love me? That's a hot one! Hey, in order to marry me he had to beg me for one year just to go out with him. And he had to beat up your Uncle Rocco and your Uncle Stephano, who tried to beat him up for asking me out. And he had to stand up to your grandfather, Felice.

"And, come to think of it, he would've had to beat up your Uncle Luigi too, except he had polio and could only write your father a nasty letter. But your father wrote a nasty letter back – all of it to win me.

"Believe me when I tell you, your father had to move heaven and earth to get me. Nonno Felice didn't want me to marry before your Aunt Ciara because she was older. So your father had to go get this barber he knew from Treviso to come down and marry Ciara. Otherwise, Grandpa insisted your father marry Ciara and forget me. Your grandfather was so orderly that a lot of problems came from it.

"Anyway, Ciara and Franco, your dear Aunt and Uncle (God rest his soul) were together because your father had to have me. So see how things work out? They were as happy as doves because God's always moving sideways, arranging things.

"No, your father loves me, Pasquale. He's just not the type to wear his heart on his sleeve. But then I'm not either. So we're a good match, really. So don't worry about it."

It was my mother's belief that she was loved by my father that most hurt and saddened me. It was also that belief which made me feel good for her. It was like the wedding ring she'd bought for herself – she had it by default, so to speak. But to her it looked nice and authentic on her finger.

✎ Ciara ✎

**In which Aunt Ciara is likened to a female
St. Francis and is explored as a special type of
Italian woman**

Although Ciara was the oldest of my mother's three
sisters, she never seemed old at all. She was too little at
4' 10" ever to be anything but a sort of loveable cross
between a Buddha and a burro.

Indeed, Ciara's small but sturdy shoulders were
designed with compassionate undertakings in mind. If
anyone had figured out that all life was suffering, it
was Ciara. And yet she said yes to it, to everything,
and in so doing carried a strange fire, a transcendent
glee. She was lit from within like a homely spirit
lantern.

From the time she was a child, Ciara had a special
gift for healing. She could soothe and she could
transmute pain into something sweet.

This worked with people, with beasts, and with
inanimate objects. Like the girl in rags who slept
unnoticed in cinders, Ciara was overlooked often –
until something hard occurred.

And then her small, dark frame was summoned.
And she came every time, her long black braid
following her to the scene of some miraculous service.

Her parents, seeing Ciara's kindness and selfless-
ness, used her to care for the family's seven younger

siblings. Endless washings, scourings, bakings, rakings and mendings became her province.

And rather than being overwhelmed by such a tax on her childhood and young womanhood, Ciara was energized – and took control of all details of life.

She had, as it turned out, an aesthetic sensibility that demanded color, beauty, spirit, proportion, fragrance, order – and above all, deliciousness. Without any formal training except being alive in Casamassima, Ciara just started knowing how to live well, with real finesse.

She knew how to clean calamari and make toys of their translucent little bones. She knew how to save their ink for dye and paintings. She knew how to pick the right mushrooms, the ones that didn't kill you. Of dandelions, she knew to make wine. Of sugar and lard she made decorative lambs that graced the Easter cakes. Her bread, woven like braids with unshelled hardboiled eggs baked into it, was beautiful; her sauces, beyond description.

She knew the Italian opera and which sopranos took risks and which ones ducked the high notes.

She knew how to get tomcats' abscesses to drain, how to wash the sheets of childbirth, when storms were coming in from the Adriatic, how artichokes should be breaded, how to list the Popes in order (including the Schism time when there were two) and when the constellations were going to constellate.

In addition to making perfect espresso, lemon ice, and eggplant parmigiana while discussing politics, Ciara knew her home turf intimately.

She'd been to so many peoples' homes, helping them can tomatoes, visiting them, watching their sick, that she knew every secret of Casamassima – from way back. And maybe even further than that.

Stunned by his sister-in-law's ubiquitous ways, my father used to tell people with consternation, "Don't mess with Ciara. She might just tell you who your grandfather really was."

But he was wrong. She wouldn't have. Ciara was not a gossip, never hurtful.

She was as compassionate a person as ever lived. Shining through everything in the world she saw the divine face of God. Even a fork she would not misuse, for somehow its very molecules had come into being through a mystery greater than she could say. That mystery was her constant meditation.

Completely humble and self-effacing, Ciara loved the shining specifics of the world. And not a one to her was deserving of scorn or dismissal.

When she was nine years old, Ciara had an experience that served to complete her training as a "Bodhisattva Italiana." Of course, it began in an ordinary way.

Her father brought home (from his job as a church sexton) an orphaned, young crow in much need of succor. Immediately charmed by such a helpless yet feisty being, Ciara gave the infant crow every drop of her attention.

In reciprocation, he thrived. In time, Benno, as he was called, began to speak loudly and raucously, squawking out Ciara's name whenever someone was about to nod off to sleep or have a profound thought which, once lost, could never be retrieved.

In short, Grandfather was damn sorry he'd brought the crow home and resolved to remedy the mistake.

Not completely insensitive to Ciara's feelings for the bird, he hit upon a plan to soften the blow and make himself look reasonable, no small feat.

He told her he'd love to have the crow continue with the family, but in order to do so, a suitable cage would need to be built outside the house near the pigeon cote – the same pigeon cote in which he kept his own racing birds. But alas, because there was no money for materials, Ciara couldn't really expect him to take food from the family's mouth to buy a few twigs, some screening, and two or three nails.

So, to be nice, he'd take the crow back to the churchyard and let him go. Free birds, it's well known, are insanely happy.

Ciara responded with insight that the crow was now tame and knew nothing about foraging; he'd starve.

"No," said Grandfather, "it's us who'll starve – waiting on him, feeding him, building him expensive living quarters. He's treated better than your Aunt Pig! Ciara, if you had the money for such a COSTLY project, I'd say 'yes'. But what can I do?"

Aunt Ciara, as my mother enjoyed telling it over and over, didn't answer back. Her eyes filled with tears and she put her head down and walked slowly and deliberately to the front door and stepped into the street.

Without looking up, she held her hand out to the air and a 100,000 lire note landed in it.

"Just like that," my mother emphasized each word, "Caravaggio came flying through the air into Ciara's fingers."

"Liar," said my father. "Caravaggio's portrait wasn't even on the 100,000 lire then. What a fiction! What a fantasy! You and your whole family are nuts."

"No," said my mother. "God never failed Ciara. He found a way to ram that crow right down our father's throat – and good for Him!"

44

In time Benno and Ciara became a familiar and welcome sight in the piazza where the women gathered to draw water and wash clothes.

Each Monday without fail the two of them appeared there to wade through the mounds of wash produced by a family of ten people. Sometimes Ciara was there for four or five hours, washing, talking, showing Benno's tricks.

One fateful day, however, Ciara's attention was diverted a little too long as she helped old Serafina Locastro empty a heavy tub filled with her thirty-five-year-old son's underwear.

When she turned back to Benno, it was too late. Always fascinated by the shining soap bubbles popping on the water's surface, Benno had fallen in while trying to peck them. He had drowned.

Ciara began to scream and cry. As soon as the other women understood why, they began screaming and crying also. Then, too, the children began screaming and crying. Not to be outdone, the dogs howled.

Ciara's grief was horrible. The women saw her dark, plain face contorted in pain, her worn little hands fumbling, unsure for once.

Ciara's hands – in water so much that she'd developed eczema that never went away – were pointing, and she was blinded by tears.

One kind woman, realizing what Ciara was pointing to, took Benno from the tub and wrapped him up in a dry pillowcase.

"I can't take your pillowcase," said Ciara thoughtfully.

"Yes, you take it. Go home. We'll bring the wash home for you today."

"No, no. You're too busy for that."

"Go on, now. Go on, Ciara. Go bury your little angel. You do something nice for him, ok? You'll feel better then, ok?"

Days went by and Ciara was inconsolable. She who had done so much for others could do nothing for herself. Nothing gave her any comfort.

Finally, still paralyzed with grief, Ciara had a dream.

In the dream, Benno himself did not appear, but rather sent his mother. Startled and pleased to see such a formidable crow backlit against a golden and radiant casement window, Ciara approached in awe.

"Come closer, Daughter," said the crow.

Obediently, Ciara walked to her. The crow, with a little flourish, showed Ciara one of her black legs – teeming with lice! Then, she laughed at Ciara's apprehension.

"Yes, Daughter," railed the crow. "The Mother is covered with Life, Life, and more Life."

Immediately Ciara woke up, changed. Her grief was over. She had seen deeper into the truth of things and had felt something move beyond birth and death. The crow's transcendent cheekiness moved on into her soul.

From that time forward, if anyone in her family was going to die, she'd dream of the Crow Mother. And though it wasn't exactly pleasant, it wasn't unpleasant either. Ciara had become a seer.

At first she was confused by the fact that God hadn't given her a consoling dream with saints or burning bushes or predictable, biblical references. But that soon passed and she realized that her experiences were probably in the tradition of St. Francis, her favorite saint. Francis had spoken with birds, clouds, water.

So everything was fine.

Benno was gone but not gone. Ciara could see his wings in the dark gloss of her own braid and in the deep iridescence of the bubbles he'd died loving.

She kept doing for others, praying unceasingly, and waiting for a new companion, one who would understand how she saw this world and the one behind it.

Fortunately, she only had to wait two more decades when Uncle Franco appeared and obliged her.

❧ Ciara e Franco ❧

In which the golden marriage of Ciara and Franco is shown in all its bittersweetness

On the strength of my father's vivid descriptions of the Ferri girls' charms, Franco Manzari, barber extraordinaire, packed up his scissors, razors, lotions, and potions and left Treviso for Casamassima.

Traveling an equivalent psychic distance between Mars and Jupiter, he abandoned the land of the rice eaters and showed up in pasta country. In years ahead his waistline would reflect this migration, but upon arrival he was a small, wiry Romeo with black hair, and brows the texture of a healthy Airedale's. The fleshy, Romantic moles on his nose completed and defined his trustworthy countenance. In every way, Franco seemed a distinctly kind and good-natured man.

And yet, after finally seeing the four Ferri girls together for the first time, he acted in a way considered by my father to be very unfriendly.

Spying on the girls as they all trooped into church one Sunday, Franco and my father saw eye-to-eye on one thing.

They both fell for Palma Ferri.

And who wouldn't?

"That one with the chestnut hair and the pouty lips and the butt like Venus, that's Palma," said my father. "She's the one I want."

"Well, I can see why," said Uncle Franco. "She's a peach, absolutely luscious."

"Yeah, well don't look too long. The one you're going to marry is Ciara, the dark one with the braid."

"No," said Franco.

"Yes, absolutely," said my father. "Ciara's the one you have to marry so I can have Palma."

"What about the other pretty one with the blonde hair, the happy-looking one?"

"No, that's Maria. She's going to marry Alfredo Riccio. They've been engaged since they were about ten-years-old."

"Oh, that's too bad. She'd be O.K. Maybe."

"Look, said my father, "you're getting Ciara. The old man's marrying them off in order or he's not marrying them off at all!"

"But Ciara's not the oldest, is she? She looks like a child."

"No, no. She's the oldest, then Maria, then Palma, and then little Gina. Believe me, Ciara's a good catch, a little dwarfy but she's well-respected."

"Well, if Palma would want me over you, why shouldn't I try?"

"Look, we have an understanding, Palma and I – *an understanding!*"

My father spoke of this understanding with some heat and with good reason. It was probably the last understanding that he and my mother would ever have.

He looked at Franco, who began to take on the appearance of a lascivious, degenerate Judas.

A few weeks passed. Uncle Franco industriously set up his barbershop and began beautifying the heads of Casamassima. What he couldn't make hair do!

One day my grandfather went in to the new tonsorial palace, and though he was three-quarters bald, Uncle Franco cut his hair in such a way that he only looked half bald. Grandfather was delighted, an emotion he'd dispensed with for thirty years.

It was Uncle Franco's golden moment. He stated his credentials and his case for marrying Palma. He spoke passionately and for a long time.

"Ciara," said my grandfather, "is who you're marrying."

"No," said Uncle Franco.

"Oh, yes," said my grandfather. "You *think* you want Palma but believe me, you don't. Palma's filled with about 20,000 devils. She's ambitious, stubborn, and self-righteous. Where these qualities come from, I have no idea. I only know if you don't marry Ciara, you can go to hell. My mind's made up. Finito."

"OK," said Uncle Franco, throwing up his hands and splashing aftershave all everywhere. "Fate speaks."

"My son-in-law," said Grandfather.

When Ciara got the news, she was happy, so happy she felt certain her prize would be taken from her. "Who am I to deserve such a wonderful new life with Franco the Barber? To have only one person to take care of every day? How will that work out? Who'll help Mother and Father with the children? Mama can't possibly manage without me."

Ciara began to feel guilty, but she needn't have. Grandfather, always the thoughtful one, made sure that Ciara and Franco would be living a few houses down the street so Ciara could still do housework for her parents and siblings. When it came to his eldest daughter, he took no gamble on losing his indentured servant.

And now there would be free haircuts and another income on which to rely "if things got bad." Grandfather was well pleased with his matchmaking prowess. Ciara was better than money in the bank.

That August, right after the arduous, annual ritual of canning the tomatoes, Ciara and Franco wed. By that time they knew each other fairly well, and Franco was quite positive he'd gotten the gem of the family. The two doted on each other, finding so many answers to life's questions answered in the other person.

Smelling sweetly of garlic, basil, and a little bit of lavender, Ciara was readied for her nuptials. Her Aunt Gioia, a talented seamstress, sewed for her an amazing little dress of heavy, cream silk and a cloche hat with long, voluminous veiling that covered Ciara like a cloud. On her little feet were white kid, lace-up boots with tiny heels.

Weeping and joking by turns, her sisters helped her dress, and presented her with a bouquet of white roses and lilies that was almost bigger than Ciara herself. A veritable rain forest of frothy ferns and white roses covered every inch of the family home.

Arriving at the flower-bedecked church with her three sisters as bridesmaids, Ciara felt for one day like a queen and said so to Franco. He began to cry and said, "You deserve all good things, Ciara. You are so good and it is I who am lucky. To think I might've wed another pains me."

By all accounts it was a perfect wedding of two ready and grateful people. And, in the sixteen years allotted them before Uncle Franco's early death, they never forgot the feelings that graced them on their wedding day.

"It's pathetic to be that happy," my mother sniffed. "It's a setup for misery. Why? Because it can't last."

She often went into this speech after Uncle Franco was gone so untimely to the other world.

"It happened with no warning," said my mother. "One morning Franco, only fifty-two years old, was going out the door to his shop when – bang! He gets this blinding headache and terrible pains in his chest. So he turns around, goes into his house, climbs upstairs, and calls for Ciara. 'Give me whiskey, a little glass' he says. She goes, pours him a little shot glass – she still has that glass, you've seen it there next to the shrine to Mary – and bingo! One sip later he's dead in her arms.

"Well, Ciara went under. They may as well have entombed her with him. She couldn't even tell you her name for a year. She collapsed. And can you imagine, she never from that day forward had another period!

"Believe me, we had to dress her for his funeral just like we dressed her for her wedding – though she was a little less cooperative. I don't mean literally. She held her arms out for us and like that – but that woman was gone. She wasn't on earth anymore.

"She'd had the dream too; the crow had come. I know because she'd told me. But we thought the crow was after Grandpa Ferri. But I guess she wasn't. You can't tell with that crow. It's tricky and it gives me the creeps, if you want the truth.

"Anyway, Uncle Franco was so popular in Casa-massima that his funeral was swamped. People loved him and they just couldn't believe he was gone. It pays to die young because then your friends are alive and can hobble in to see you. When you're old, forget it!

"And these people had lost a lot. Franco could take somebody who looked like a thistle field was lodged on his head and snip, snip, here and there – ah, suddenly – *bellisimo*. They mourned that one with good reason!"

53

At this juncture, my mother would go to the massive writing desk and pull out some photographs of Uncle Franco in his casket. As a child, just knowing they were in the drawer gave me heart palpitations.

"Look, look at him," she'd admonish me. "So rosy and natural and fresh; he never suffered. What *is* life? What *is* death? He had so many flowers they spilled out into the street. Your Aunt Ciara, she walked through it like through a dream. What a cheat. What a horror. She's never been really happy for one moment since he died."

And it was partly true. Many a time I went to stay with Aunt Ciara to cheer her up, to no avail. She'd iron and cry and reminisce about her time with Franco.

In later years, when Grandma had died, Ciara was sucked right back into her father's home to care for him. There, too, I visited her frequently and heard her marvel at the circular quality of her life.

"I ended up back here, just like I never left," she said, "just like Uncle Franco had never been alive, like we never existed together."

"But I know you did," I'd say fervently.

"Yes, me too," she'd respond after thinking a bit.

And sometimes, in her very last years, she'd smile like someone with a marvelous secret, lift her head to listen to the birds outside, and sigh with contentment.

"It won't be that long now," she'd say to Uncle Franco. "They're talking about us. I can hear them."

❧ "When You Close Your Eyes ❧ For the Last Time"

In which Grandpa Ferri's professional life as a Sexton and misanthrope comes to light

Grandfather Ferri was uninterested in Man and God. He did like trees, pigeons, and his guitar, which he played on feast days, alone in his room.

Like most Italian family men he made every effort to avoid his family whenever possible, either by going to work or by hanging around with other family men. In Grandfather's case, he bypassed even the latter and substituted his racing pigeons for male bonding. Males, after all, were still people and therefore problematic.

But the pigeons, whenever he told them, raced through the heavens by their own power as fast as they could – and left him alone, grounded, and in control. They were, to this end, ideal companions for him, not to mention edible in a pinch.

Grandfather's favorite maxim was, "When you close your eyes for the last time, who are you going to tell your good times to?" He said this frequently or whenever people suggested that his misanthropic behavior was cheating him (and them) out of life's many joys.

But Grandfather cared little for such frivolous suggestions. He, perhaps since childhood, had practiced "the attitude of Pragmatic Disdain." It was not, I'm sorry to report, original to him. Its roots were in the culture, in a field upon which Grandfather had grazed since birth. (In his case, however, he may have overgrazed.)

Such an attitude, cherished by so many Italian men and women, could be picked up on any given day in a thousand responses to a thousand ideas put forth by their more hopeful, idealistic counterparts – those who were ritually sacrificed to the Pragmatic Disdain god.

If, for example, some hapless soul came into a group of practicing Pragmatic Disdainers and announced, "Hey, my son Gianni's going to Rome, to the university to study. He just got accepted...." That was their cue.

The Pragmatic Disdainers could respond with one or more of the following retorts. They always began with "What!"

"What! There aren't any more books for him to read right here? What Rome? Rome, my ass."

"What! He can't find a job like a decent kid? What's he running away from? What Rome? Rome, my ass."

"What! He can't find a nice boyfriend right here? Ha ha ha! What Rome? Rome, *his* ass!"

To be one up, even on the other Pragmatic Disdainers, Grandfather didn't hang around with them or bother talking to anyone if he could help it. This, he found, cut out ninety-nine percent of the frippery others might try engaging him in. He saved a lot of time not having to be witty. Above all, he didn't really approve of the "light swearing" which hardcore Pragmatic Disdainers invoked for their humor. He did not want to refer to his ass in public.

Grandfather was at heart a real Puritan and a very single-minded person. He married Grandmother at sixteen, produced his eight children over a twenty-six year span, and ate two hardboiled eggs for lunch – with salt – every day of his working life.

By the time my exhausted, heartbroken grandmother died at sixty-four, he'd already known her over fifty years. Unknown to him, he had almost three more decades to be a widower, a state he accepted without much emotion at all. He'd put in his time, done his duty by her, and they were both now free for individual pursuits. Maybe she was a little bit freer, but hey, he didn't hold it against her.

His children, especially his daughters, saw it differently. To them, he'd killed their beloved mother with too many children, too much work, and too little compassionate attention. Though they all felt like this, only my mother in her characteristically blunt way ever brought it up – and at Grandmother's funeral, to boot.

For this, Grandfather did not forgive her. He did, however, appear to. Her focaccia business was a major factor behind this feigned attitude. Palma had money "if things got bad" – and that fear was at the bottom of his whole being.

Still, he had felt it within his fatherly right to give his daughter Palma as much grief as possible over her desire to wed my father. He watched her like a hawk and whenever he suspected she'd seen my father, all hell broke loose. He, on separate occasions, locked her out of the house, chased her up into a cherry tree, and pushed her out the front door wearing only her black slip. Morality lectures, he also provided her with, free of charge, explaining in great detail that she was little more than a stray cat in season, devoid of sense and religion.

As soon as these storms passed, my mother went right back to visiting my father and slamming her focaccia dough around like she was Cleopatra at the helm of her barge.

Grandfather wasn't winning at that campaign and it irked him to no end.

Each morning at first light, Grandfather took his little lunch of eggs, olives, and coffee and walked through sleepy Casamassima to the church and its grounds. As sexton, he was in charge of keeping the church building in good repair and also with planting, pruning, and generally gardening its lands into fruition. Additionally, he was to tend to the adjoining convent's gardens.

The convent, run by Franciscan nuns, housed both the nuns and their charges, a number of deaf children who were learning sign language, lip reading, and in some cases, embroidery techniques.

To support themselves, the orphaned children among this group embroidered sheets and sent them off to Rome to be sold. The "non-orphaned" children concentrated on learning to sign and if capable, to speak. But they didn't have to embroider.

This class division irritated Grandfather, who felt keenly that the "non-orphaned," "non-embroiderers" were lazy rotters. He was piqued especially by play periods that were given only to children with parents.

This disparity, though, was one of his profession's only thorns.

Usually entranced and fascinated by immersion in the horticultural splendors of his job, Grandfather never complained about his duties. A true nature spirit and wild man, he could graft peach branches onto pear trees, get gorgeous fruit from formerly barren, sad trees within a few seasons.

At his fragrant work, Grandfather was reborn in light and became his name, Felice. He was completely and utterly happy in this gardening paradise. Man nauseated; nature refreshed.

At such times he understood heaven and religion perfectly. He was beyond all dualities, free from bothersome ties to the temporal. He was Jove, great Jupiter grandly sprinkling a little energy here, a little there – and all nature bloomed out, lush and delightful. If by some miracle he could've been glimpsed by his family at these mythic moments, they would have been shocked.

There he would've frisked on delicate golden hooves, their grumpy patriarch, now transformed into a great white bull with hyacinthine curls, pawing and snorting ecstatically in his leafy bower of bliss.

Grandfather's cherished dream, it turned out, was to someday go to America, and own more land than the priest he worked for. Then, he thought, he'd be truly happy.

One day after hearing Grandfather complain about the poorly treated orphan embroiderers for her whole life, Aunt Gina, a child herself, insisted on accompanying her father to his work to see them.

Why this fascination had emerged puzzled Grandfather enough to entertain taking her. Usually he wouldn't have given a second thought to dismissing her. But this was curious. Something told him to pay attention.

Aunt Gina, a serious and gangly child with the perspicacious gaze of an owl, bothered Grandfather. She was obviously going to be an intellectual, probably was going to need eyeglasses, a bad, minor expense – and worst of all, maybe she'd insist on going to a university some day – a huge *major* expense.

It was this last that bothered Grandfather most. He had Gina earmarked as the spinster who'd take care of him in his old age and it rankled him to think of her getting away.

Whatever he was thinking regarding Gina in the future, on this particular day he decided to honor her request and satisfy his own curiosity in so doing.

He let her trot along beside him to work like a grim, bowlegged calf that never fattened up. Gina trailed her father, silently nursing her own thoughts.

When they arrived at the convent to meet the children, seven-year-old Gina stood stupefied and then, with uncharacteristic force, hit herself in the forehead, a corrective gesture.

"What the hell," she blurted out, shocking the nuns and flooring Grandfather, who for some reason was starting to become giddy.

"They've *got* ears! They've *got* ears, the same as everyone else!"

"What's the matter with you?" shouted Grandfather. "Why wouldn't they have ears?"

"Because I thought they wouldn't. You explained they couldn't hear."

"Hey, I never said they didn't have ears."

At this display, the nuns didn't know what to do. Then, one of them began to sniffle and cry, protectively herding the children inside away from Gina.

At these tears, Grandfather began to laugh, laugh like a hyena. Gina's literal mindedness was so ridiculous, so stupidly innocent – yet it seemed to the nuns like she was full of malice, a little monster of depravity.

"No ears," laughed Grandfather. "No ears. Boo-hoo-hoo. No play period. Only favoritism, fancy sheets, and hypocritical bitches. That's what they got around here."

From that day forth, Grandfather had a soft spot in his heart for Gina. She was an arrow he'd shot into the target without having to aim. She was a carrier pigeon who delivered a fantastic message and came home to him.

She had even, quite possibly, provided one of those good times that Grandfather wouldn't be able to tell anybody about when he closed his eyes for the last time.

❧ Aunt Mary's "Philosofia" ❧

In which a carpe diem feminine presence is evoked

If Aunt Ciara was Good Friday, the Holy Passion, and
a glimpse of the otherworld, Aunt Mary was Easter
Sunday, the Ascension, and this world all the way.
Academically, you might say that Ciara was Plato and
that Mary was Aristotle.

She came, my grandmother assured us, streaming
into the world like spring sun and never gave anyone a
moment's worry – not for fifty-three years until she
reached a crabby menopause. But how far in the future
that seemed when she was a golden-haired young lady
of twenty-six, svelte and sophisticated as a calla lily.

Aunt Mary's emblem, her family fame, her signature, was a fabulous sponge cake filled with syrupy
fruit, apricot liqueur, and whipped cream – topped
with syrupy fruit, apricot liqueur, and whipped cream.

For any celebration or just for the hell of it,
because she so enjoyed making it, the wondrous
sponge cake would appear.

It weighed about forty pounds in its stocking feet
and was guaranteed (like some sophisticated weapon
which keeps exploding after it has entered the body) to
go down deceptively easy and kill you in a half hour.

The first time the sponge cake manifested was at
little Gina's First Communion feast. Determined to
celebrate and rival this youngest sister's initial taste of
Jesus, Mary searched out the best bakers in

Casamassima for a special recipe – and finally decided on the spongy extravaganza.

When Gina gangled radiantly home from church in her stiff white communion dress, the sacred host still stuck to the roof of her mouth – it was a sin to chew it – she was presented with a white, ribbon-festooned seat of honor at the family table.

And the orgy commenced. It was a simple meal really – one consisting of green salad with gorgonzola crumbles, homemade cavatelli in tomato sauce with meat balls, sausage, and braciole; baked sole, shrimp, a few roasted chickens, mushrooms stuffed with eggs, basil, and cheese; eggplant parmigiana, ripe melon wrapped in prosciutto, provolone, and boiled ham slices; olives, figs, sugared grapes, green beans sautéed with garlic and onions, three kinds of bread and rolls, sparkling wine (Malvasia di Lecce), coffee, fifteen kinds of cookies, lemon, chocolate, and orange-flavored nougat candy; almonds, anisette, gelato, and fancy chocolates shaped like starfish, sea horses and Poseidon.

Slyly, Aunt Mary held back with her pyrotechnical confection until the very last moment.

Noticing finally that anyone still left alive and able to breathe a little was about to call it quits and stop eating, she burst triumphantly into the room to proffer her elephantine tidbit.

"So who's going to ruin Gina's big day by refusing to have a piece of her Communion cake?" asked Aunt Mary, plunking it down in front of big-eyed Gina.

Silence. Worshipful silence.

The cake drew the family into its spell. They looked at it and it looked back with its come-hither frosting. Finally, my father held up his fork.

"Not me. I'm celebrating Gina's being brainwashed by religious fanatics with a big piece of cake."

"Shame. Shame," said my grandmother, crossing herself.

But everyone else laughed and Aunt Mary helped Gina cut the first huge slices – one for Gina and one for my father.

Then, there was no stopping anyone else.

"Just a little piece."

"No, no, I shouldn't. Just a taste, just a sliver. No, a little bigger than THAT! How stingy!"

"Well, why not! Gina's not going to have another First Communion right away."

"Not for me, please. I couldn't eat one more bite. Just give me, somebody, half of yours. We'll split it – somebody, please…. Oh, forget it. Give me my own slice."

It was for moments like this that Aunt Mary lived. Her very nature was one of overindulging her loved ones, bathing them with every sweetness she could find.

It was she who kept fresh flowers in the house, made sure her sisters had fancy shoes, gloves, combs, barrettes, hats, and cosmetics if a social occasion arose where they needed them.

If she could've ordered pumps with goldfish swimming in the heels or put on a Carmen Miranda hat made of marzipan fruit, she would have done it.

A true decadent, she lived to prove that the parts of something should eclipse the whole, that only excess meant you really had enough.

For her, life was very like a big, huge bowl of cherries and nothing struck her too seriously. She couldn't see pits, worms, or canker spots.

From the time she was a child she was followed around by a little boy named Alfredo who found her to be the most exotic and fascinating individual in the world. He had hit upon the idea of marrying her since laying eyes on her – and that was fine with her. His *excessive* fondness suited her perfectly.

Alfredo, who even as a boy looked like an earnest, rather feeble-minded Rudolph Valentino, gave everything he ever got for himself to Mary. He even gave her his pure white canary with one black feather, a most coveted treasure. The thing with giving her gifts was – and Alfredo seemed to figure it out early – that you could be sure she appreciated them and that she'd reciprocate a thousand fold.

When Mary was eighteen she found a temporary job in a fireworks factory. The reason the job was temporary was because the factory blew up one night about an hour after Mary and the other girls who worked there had left for the evening.

The huge explosion that ripped through the fireworks factory stunned Casamassima. Thank God, everyone said, the girls had left. Else, oh! Who could have faced the results!

When Alfredo found that his inamorata had nearly been rocketed into the sky like a Roman candle, he ran down the street to her house and demanded to see her. He knocked at the front door and hollered piteously.

Looking out the window of her balcony at Alfredo, all upset and crazy in the moonlit aftermath of the explosion, struck Mary as funny.

She was laughing when Grandfather, twice roused from his beauty sleep – first by errant fireworks and then by a lovesick boy – started cursing. He had to get up early the next day, he explained at a volume that rivaled the exploding factory.

"What must a man do this night to be left alone, to sleep before going to work? You two have driven me crazy long enough with this love business! It's time to put an end to it once and for all. You better just get married as soon as possible!"

With that, he slammed the door in Alfredo's face and chased Mary, her laughter trailing behind her, to bed.

Suddenly, and it was just Aunt Mary's luck, she was out of a job but into a husband.

Thereafter, if anyone stopped her on the street and told her how happy they were to hear of her narrow escape from the fiery mishap, she'd just chuckle away. They were overreacting and overdramatizing, she knew for a fact.

For Mary, life lay before her like an unopened present. If factories blew up, she'd never be in them anyway, so no congratulations were needed. Wasn't that perfectly obvious?

Such a blessed existence would be true of her young life as well as of her coming years. Some three decades after the fireworks escapade Aunt Mary was on the Andrea Doria's last successful voyage, the one before it sank to the bottom of the Atlantic Ocean.

"It's a shame, such a pretty ship," Aunt Mary would lament as she served up cannoli and coffee to her sisters and Alfredo. "I'm glad I could at least keep this souvenir."

Everyone else was glad too, believing it was a collector's item and valuable. Very few people they knew possessed an Andrea Doria ashtray in the shape of a life preserver, but Aunt Mary did.

❧ Bibi e Mal Occhio ❧

In which the supernatural underpinnings of
Pugliese culture are recalled

"That's only for Sicilians," my mother scoffed at the
Death Sisters, who had come to tell her that Anita
Fonticone across the street had died from being cursed.
"I don't believe in all that crap. Who put it on her?"

"Palma," confided Anna Posa, "that's the thing. It
was Trombone Iaia – and your sister Ciara was right
there with Anita when it happened!"

"What? My sister, Ciara? When was this?"

"About one year ago. See, Ciara and Anita were
walking back from the piazza, arm in arm, giving little
Bibi her daily walk, when Trombone came out of
nowhere, scowling. Well, Bibi began barking at him.
That little dog loved Anita so." (Pause. Tears. Rolling
of eyes.) "Oh, excuse me. It's hard to believe she's
gone. So, barking – you know, protectively. Dear little
black Bibi. And Trombone, God help us, the ugliest
man alive...."

"It's his nose," volunteered Fiora. "The veins on it
look like some pattern only a devil could've left. They
stick out a mile."

"So does his whole nose," my mother interjected.
"He's not called Trombone for no reason. Get to it,
Anna. Then what?"

"Oh, he makes a gesture towards Bibi with his cane,
like he's going to hit her for barking. And then, he just

stops and looks at Anita, she was *so* beautiful." (Pause. Tears. Rolling of eyes.) "And he says, 'You're next!'"

"'You're next'?" asked my mother. "That's what he said? That's it?"

"Next to DIE is what he meant," explained Anna confidentially. "It was in that moment he gave her the *mal occhia.*"

"Maybe he meant he was going to hit her with the cane next?" my mother offered, a halfhearted defense.

"No, no, no. He hadn't hit Bibi *first*, so he could hardly hit Anita *next!*"

"Hey, he's maybe senile? Maybe he forgot to hit Bibi but thought he did."

"No," said Anna Posa with supernatural insight. "He in that moment signed her death warrant. Listen, you know how she and her husband had never been able to have children?"

"Yes, I do remember that."

"Well, right after Trombone's attack, suddenly Anita's pregnant for the first time at thirty-six. Her periods stop, and she and Costanzo are so happy, they're crazy. But then, nine months go by, Anita gets big as a house, bigger and bigger and no baby. Ten months go by and what do you think? Anita" (sob) "goes to Bari – to the *good* hospital there – and she dies. She gave birth, not to a baby, but to some horrible growth!"

They all crossed themselves and kissed their fingers as Anna finished her tale with triumph, somewhat like a brilliant trial lawyer who'd proved his case.

"I don't like these stories," my mother declared. "They make me have bad dreams. You really think Trombone did it?"

"Hey, believe what you want. I know he did. He always had impure thoughts towards her, that mean old lecher. How many prayers have I uttered for his salvation after his sweet wife died. When she was on her last legs, I'd sit with her, trying to cheer her up – and Trombone would be looking out the window at Anita, God rest her soul. I'd be praying unceasingly for his eternal soul and for Francesca's pains, and he'd be praying that Anita would drop something and bend over. He couldn't take his eyes off her!"

"It was her black, black hair," Fiora said. "He couldn't resist that blackness. It was like looking at his own soul – in a dark mirror."

"Oh, you're right," said Anita. "That's what it was. But Anita herself was so good. Only her hair was dark, not her. She was GOOD!"

"Yes, yes, she was," everyone agreed. "We'd better get home and make something special for her wake."

After the Death Sisters left, my mother, somehow against her will, got madder and madder at Trombone. She summoned Ciara who agreed that he had told Anita she was 'next.' But Ciara, with infuriating objectivity, wasn't sure what he'd meant. Too late, though.

It was enough for my mother, who loved animals so much, to begin to dwell on Trombone's menacing Bibi with his cane. She commenced her own case against him.

He was an odd one, all right; she had to admit that. And she had never liked the way he looked at her or other pretty women.

"Old, ugly farts" who thought they had rights to look at young, beautiful women really annoyed my mother – just as a general rule.

But Trombone had an extra sinister quality to him. The rumors were he had beaten his wife Francesca's head in with a brick and that she had the indentation to prove it. The fact that she changed the part in her hair a lot didn't help matters much either. Such a manic and suspicious attention to her head's demarcations invited speculative intensity.

Many a neck in Casamassima grew stiff and sore craning to look at the top of Francesca Iaia's head. That she was a tall woman thwarted lots of good investigative work and further increased peoples' disgust with Trombone. He put them through so much trouble! He must have been guilty.

My mother, as she mulled over Trombone's character, finally hit upon the two memories that had stuck in her craw the most. Trombone had once savagely ventured that her focaccia tasted "a little dry," and on another occasion he had told her little brother Luigi (who'd had polio) to "quit limping and walk like a man."

She was (now that she had remembered these two suppressed gems) glad the Death Sisters had come over to jog her recollection. Trombone, by God, would not escape retribution.

He had killed Anita Fonticone as sure as if he had shot her with a cannon.

On the third and last night of Anita Fonticone's wake, my mother and her sisters went across the street to "pay their respects" and see their poor neighbor one last time. As for her husband Costanzo, they took him some cash, focaccia, and cookies filled with fig paste – the kinds of things coveted by widowers everywhere.

As they entered the crowded parlor where Anita was laid out, they expelled a collective gasp. There on the carpet near the head of Anita's coffin sat the loyal little Bibi, guarding her mistress in death as she had always done in life. It was a heartbreaking sight – little Bibi looking for all the world like she was receiving mourners, her small, black form leaning snugly against Anita's box.

For a split second my mother felt it would be very natural to offer the cash, bread, and fig pastries to Bibi and skip Costanzo. (Hadn't the dog been with Anita more hours out of her life than he had?) But forget that.

It was not merely the image of the faithful and elegantly sad, vigilant Bibi which evoked the Ferri girls' gasp. No. No.

It was the sight of Trombone Iaia gently patting the top of Bibi's unprotesting head as he made to bend over and kiss Anita's forehead...or was it her lips...or was it the place where her hairline began, that seductive limnal area between her dark hair and white skin?

No one would ever be sure.

My mother let out a shriek that froze the entire room in its tracks and Trombone's lips in mid-pucker.

"Get, get, get away from that girl," my mother screamed at the startled, dazed Trombone. "Get away from her and that dog or I'll throw you into the street myself. Right now!"

The roomful of mourners sucked in their breath and covered their mouths. Their eyes went back and forth from my mother's livid, gorgeous, Gorgon's face to Trombone's old, confused mask.

He looked at Anita longingly one last time, and then back to my mother's obdurate eyes. His own strange eyes filled bitterly with tears and he left as fast as his old skeleton could clank out of the spinning room.

My mother stood clenching and unclenching her fists, staring at the place where he'd stood moments before. She too was confused, however, as to what had ensued.

The Death Sisters, who'd been surveying the goings on from their prominent perch near Costanzo's ancient, weeping mother, were atwitter. As they watched, Old Signora Fonticone was clutching at the air, about to pass out. Costanzo had fallen to his knees with grief. And Bibi was nervously licking her lips and eyeing the fig pastries with unmistakable distress. It had really paid off to attend Anita's wake all three evenings.

"Palma certainly gave him some hell," whispered Anna. "She seems bewitched. What's going on with *her*?"

"God help her," said Fiora. "What if he gives her the evil eye next? She's gone out on a limb there, wouldn't you say?"

"It would be too obvious," reasoned Maria. "Everybody would remember what happened here tonight. The old monster would hang himself."

"Ah. Good point," the others agreed. "Palma seems like she handled this just right. It's such a lucky thing we drew the whole matter to her attention."

❧ Uncle Stroonze and the ❧ Cat's Tonsillectomy

In which Uncle Stroonze does the wrong thing with the wrong eating utensil

For months after Anita Fonticone's wake, my mother embarked on an "anti" hunger campaign on the behalf of Bibi. She ran back and forth across the street many times, warning Costanzo not to neglect Bibi's dinners, snacks, treats, and walks, now that Anita was gone.

Something had been triggered in her, my father and I noticed, and she was more than usually dedicated to ministering to the neighborhood's pets, especially our own. What her sister Mary did for people, my mother did for creatures – petting, encouraging, and fattening them up.

Noticing that the two dogs Regina and Goffo were beginning to resemble sausages and that the African parrot, Papa, seemed to have double chins under his beak, my father became alarmed. The crisis peaked when his friend, a slightly manic-depressive dentist named Graceffo asked my father what kind of dogs Regina and Goffo were.

"Why, they're greyhounds," said my father.

"Ah, no!" said Signore Graceffo. "They *were* greyhounds. Underneath, perhaps somewhere – maybe greyhounds again sometime, eh?"

75

That sly comment by a perceptive madman pushed my father to fight for the pets' rights to regain their figures. He embarked on his own campaign.

"They're going to drop dead, they're so fat!" my father would gripe. "Popo [the cat] dwarfs the over-stuffed chair he's on right now! Is this kindness, Palma? To make him blow up and die?"

"Hey, if he dies on a full stomach, I'll have done my duty by him and rest in peace. What do you want from me?"

"Stop feeding him so much!"

"Oh, no! And end up like that cheapskate, Uncle Stroonze? No thanks. I feed what I love, and spend whatever it takes to make these poor animals happy. I'm not like Stroonze, and that's enough for me – cheap bastard!"

"What did Uncle Stroonze do again? Tell me what he did," I'd plead. "Tell me, Mama."

"I've told you fifty million times. He took his cat's tonsils out with a spoon!"

"But why is that cheap? If he wasn't attached to the cat, he wouldn't have tried to help her, right?"

"What 'attached'? 'Attached' my ass! He did it because he wouldn't pay the veterinarian for a little throat medicine. The cat just needed a little dose of medicine."

"Cats don't even have tonsils," explained my father to me with absolute authority, an authority I chose to ignore for the sake of the ongoing narrative action.

"But how did he get the cat to open her mouth, Mama? Cats don't usually just open up and let you poke around in them with spoons. Was the cat in a coma?"

"Hey, I don't know what it was in. Your Grandfather Ferri's the one who came back and made everyone sick with the whole stupid story!"

"But what good's a story without details? Was the cat comatose? Was she hypnotized?"

"What? What are you worried about here, the cat or your entertainment?"

"Both, I suppose! I like cats. I like details."

"Good, then. Here are some details for you about your beloved Uncle Stroonze who was so cheap he squeaked when he walked! For starters, he lived way out on the outskirts of the town exactly like an animal – no, worse, animals live with more luxuries – in a hovel.

"He wouldn't even let your poor Great-Aunt Sanda have a sofa or a real bed frame or come into town to church. The worst of it was when she wanted a little plaster shrine of Our Lady Of Fatima when she was dying to keep by her mattress-side. See, I didn't say 'bedside' because of keeping in mind *details* for you.

"Well, she had to promise if he got it for her and she happened by a miracle to get better, she'd pay him back for it, every penny. Well, ha-ha, he never got his money out of her on that one. She died and fixed him. God, he just reminds me of Trombone Iaia to a T! He never deserved to have a woman so much as *speak* to him, let alone *marry* him.

"Okay. So, she's dead and then he's left out there like some werewolf in the woods –"

"Stop! I love that image, Mama. Go slower."

"Yeah, you would. So he's reverting back to a primitive state – he and your Grandfather Felice are just alike in this, by the way. If they could turn into wolves, they'd do it. And, uh, now he's got nobody. His

77

kids left and so forth. Only stray cats and wild dogs are sticking around him at that point.

"So, the one cat, the Tonsil Cat, she's the one he happens to be 'doctoring' (hmmph!) when Grandpa Ferri trots out finally to see him. And he's got hardly any food, no clean clothes, no ambition – that's the big problem here – and he suddenly is the great cat surgeon. And he spoons out the poor cat's tonsils, and of course she dies. Who'd want to hang around long with Stroonze, anyway? Poor cat."

"Wait," I interjected. "If she could've, she'd have asked him for a little statuette of Bast, the cat goddess to look at while she was lingering – just like Sanda wanted Our Lady of Fatima."

"Where the hell does *that* come from?"

"Egypt."

"What?"

"We Catholic women have the Virgin Mother. Cats have Bast. Back in Egypt they did."

"I don't care about any of that nonsense. Do you want me to finish the story or not? You read too much!"

"Yes, I do. Sorry."

"God, you're so hard to tell anything to, Pasquale, just like your father. Uh...so, the poor cat dies of an infection from Stroonze's helpful interference, and your grandfather and he get into a big fight –"

"I don't think I can listen to this part again and live," said my father matter-of-factly. "Please, cease."

"No, tell it, Mama. What did they fight about? Was Grandpa Ferri upset by his brother's crassness, his cruelty to the cat? Aunt Sanda's wretched life?"

"Hell, no. He was upset about the spoon! It was one of our good spoons, Grandma Ferri's good dowry spoons – and Grandpa recognized it. Stroonze had lifted it once when he'd come to dinner, thinking never to have been called on it! What do you think of THAT?"

"Silver... I see, as you say it... A beautiful filigree spoon pattern —"

"That's it for you!" yelled my mother, now completely frustrated. "The point of this story is not how good the spoon looked. The point is that they both missed the point. The point is there's no point to men like that. And that's why I vowed as a little girl, listening to that story, always to be generous to creatures and to make sure I could buy whatever the hell I wanted with my own money. You can be sure when I die I'm not asking any man for a little chalk statue, and also if I want to feed Popo 'til he's got a little meat on his bones, I will damn well do it, get it?"

My father and I looked at each other. We got it. My mother had to overfeed all the animals in the world because men were asocial, untrustworthy, petty ogres who took care of themselves first and left women, children and all other living beings in the world the scraps, if that.

By liberal feeding, she evened the score in favor of Life and the Feminine, both of which she represented with self-appointed fervor. If you looked at her closely enough, a garland of skulls would form around her neck — all of them men's skulls.

Unlike the goddess Kali, however, my mother had a second garland, a special one, with fat little animals and women and children, and they were fine and healthy. These were in her special care and she flaunted her prejudice for them freely.

As individuals she did not care for them so much. But on principle she'd help them out as long as they

79

seemed oppressed by the masculine – or even slightly undernourished.

❧ Pasquale's Spy Mission ❧

In which I come of age under a closed shutter

The day after the "Uncle Stroonze discussion" my mother increased her fretting about the fact that Costanzo Fonticone might not be tending to Bibi properly. To that end she sent me out on a spy mission to follow them on their daily walk. If I noticed that he only let Bibi pee a few measly times and then yanked her back home unceremoniously, or if Bibi wanted to linger and sniff and he yelled at her and made her self-conscious, I was to report this.

As usual, I trotted off to do my mother's bidding, no matter how ridiculous.

Following them surreptitiously was fine for a while, but suddenly it dawned on me that a couple things were wrong. The first was that Costanzo walked like a zombie and that without Bibi to tend to – a duty he obviously felt he needed to shoulder – he probably would never have left his house at all. He was a walking depression: shriveled, shuffling and shocked. The more I watched little Bibi look up at his face, searching for signs of life and relationship in his eyes, the worse I felt. They both were lost without Anita.

And Anita I began to dwell on, too. Where was she now, really? How did Costanzo stand it, knowing she was just outside of town a little, all dressed up and confined in that marble chest of drawers, the mausoleum? And not home in her bed frisking with him or worrying about life's little dramas?

My mother, I felt, was herself capable of missing quite a few points in life. Costanzo did care about Bibi. He didn't stint her walk at all. He stayed out with her a long time to avoid going home. Obviously, he was doing something for Anita in taking care of the dog. Bibi was a link between them and he was honoring it. Costanzo, though a man, was capable of love.

The second wrong thing was that I began to suspect my parents had wanted me out of the house so they could talk about me behind my back. My mother had been on my case a little more than usual since I'd asked her about Uncle Stroonze and the spoon. What was she thinking about me?

I decided to return home posthaste and spy on the spymaster, letting myself move silently and with rampant curiosity.

"Pasquale's a weird child," my mother was saying as I arrived home, flattening myself under the open window nearest the front door. "She's too much with the books – and that she gets from your family. It's no good. It separates a person from life to be that way."

"Oh, life. You and life," my father snuffed. "Pasquale's just after the narrative moment. Pasquale's got an inner life. She's artistic, is all. She wants to write about things, to experience things deeply!"

"Well, she needn't write or study me and my family and air our dirty laundry. That's private. It's nobody's business but our own. And I'll tell you another thing. Her emotions aren't natural. You can't tell what she's really thinking or feeling!"

"Yeah, I'll go along with that," agreed my father, suddenly seeming to desert my defense. "She hides a lot. She doesn't open herself up. But come on, Palma –

why would she? Do you ever give her any praise, any kind word?"

"What! Now it's my fault Pasquale's like she is! Hey, she's fed good and has good clothes, and she always knows her mother's here in this house working her tail off for her! What kind word does she need more than that?"

"Something kind can't hurt. Pasquale's very sensitive."

"Pasquale's sensitive, all right," my mother confirmed with malice. "She's also morbid, always dwelling on vampires and werewolves and the like. Remember the time she thought she was dying of rabies? You had to assure her she wasn't because no dog had bit her. No bat had chewed on her!"

"Well, sure. She's a little hypochondriacal..."

"Yeah? And where's that come from? Not me. I don't have time to think about being sick. That's from you she gets that stuff."

"Oh, no, Palma. No. My sisters don't have Death Crows appearing to them, or pig children, or money flying out of the sky into their hands! She gets this from hanging around with you and Ciara. She idolizes Ciara, you know!"

"Yes, I know," cried my mother, strangely hurt, tears flooding her voice. "Ciara's the one she goes to. After all I do for her! Ciara's the one she treats like a mother! Ciara's the one she loves!"

"Hey, Palma. Ciara *likes* Pasquale. She listens to her for hours."

"Well, I don't have time to like her or listen to her for hours. I have to work to feed her, work to keep everything going."

My father, I could now imagine, pursed his lips and shook his head. The discussion was going to move from me to a more personal topic – him – and I could tell he wasn't going to go there if he could avoid it.

"Pasquale's got good qualities underneath," he finally asserted. "I'm not sure she's exactly nice or forthcoming or has her feet on the ground in any significant way. But she's intelligent. Maybe she'll pull out!"

"Yeah?" railed my mother. "Well, I think she's afraid to be alive is what I think. You can't live in stories. Not in them or off them. You have to live in the real world eventually, and I don't know how in hell Pasquale's going to do that! She's off the beam!"

With that said, my mother clapped the shutter above my head closed with a loud snap, leaving me standing there, still pressed to the stucco of our house. She hadn't seen me.

It was shocking, to say the least, to hear my parents try to finalize my character and my future. But to do it through the filter of their own problems seemed somehow misguided and absolutely wrong. And it certainly hurt.

My mother's attack on books and on the life of the imagination also floored me. The one thing I thought she'd liked about me was that I loved listening to her stories. And come to find out, she even suspected that!

And her jealousy of Aunt Ciara! My goodness, she'd pushed me off on her from the time I was an infant. Why wouldn't I love Ciara? Why didn't my mother appreciate that love? Was it because Ciara loved selflessly and my mother never could? Could it be she resented even her own sister?

My head spun round with all the faults I'd been assigned. Was I doomed, as they feared? Me who wasn't even "nice?"

My father had managed to defend me a little, hadn't he? Could I reclaim a shred of worth from his belief that I was "artistic"? And what did *that* mean? Would I end up with my ear cut off, living with prostitutes and people who drank absinthe and stayed up all night?

What a day! What had started off as an inquiry into Costanzo's life and motives had turned suddenly into an inquiry into mine! My mother had set us both up, actually.

I vowed then and there – under the sign of the closed shutter – to share nothing of my astute insights into Costanzo's grief-life and his respect for Bibi's right to a liberal walk with lots of will-o'-the-wisp peeing.

My mother wouldn't believe me anyway. Her spy missions were forgone conclusions, guilt already assigned.

My father was essentially right. Until a kind word came my way from my mother, I'd continue to guard my inner life and not share it fully with her – or with him, either!

And I would write about everything and everybody and prove to myself and the world that stories are absolutely what we live in. And that people who don't know that are the most unreal and deluded people of all.

Afraid to be alive?! That was a good one. Why, for me to be alive in my parents' world I had to hide, jump through hoops, invoke subterfuge and spin more deftly than a dervish.

To be alive, I noticed, I went through considerable trouble. And to be alive fully, I chronicled and noticed and interviewed that trouble until it turned to something else – until it turned to meaning! Didn't my mother know why I was buoyed up by stories?

My mother had had her youthful time of declaration and reaction against the cruelties that she knew to fight, and now I must have mine. If her anger and my father's depression were two bars on the prison of my life, well, it was now up to me to remove them – or at least thread the ivy of my stories around them, transmuting them a little.

That must just be the way it goes, I surmised. Strong Italian mothers make strong Italian daughters – not by helping or gently reinforcing them, but by pissing them off, ignoring them, and misrepresenting them so the daughters have to get mad and kick some butt. And the butt they have to kick is their mother's!

I'd been way too respectful of my mother, that was the problem. Too much yes-Mama-this and sorry-Mama-that. Well, no more!

While I was standing under the shutter, coming of age, vowing to write about the most embarrassing minutiae of my mother's family life, my grandmother hobbled by on her way home.

"Hey Pasquale, why are you standing there under the shutter?" she shouted over, perplexed.

"I'm mad at my mother," I yelled back. "I know she's your daughter and all that, but she's got some harsh ways."

"Eh, si," said my grandmother. "That's one way of putting it. That's nice. The way I put it is she's a pain in the ass. From the moment she was born, a pain in the ass."

"Well, it's good to hear *you* say it," I said, surprised.

"Hey, why lie? That's the way I raised her: stubborn as a bull. She'd make even Jesus bite his nails."

❧ Uncle Luigi's Polio ❧

In which Uncle Luigi is turned into
a eunuch by his doting mother and sisters

"Walnut water," decided Ianine Vanacore with eerie
confidence. "Bathe it in walnut water in the morning,
at noon, and at night. And make sure you pray when
you do it, too!"

Then she left the house where my grandmother, my
mother, and my two oldest aunts were crying over my
uncle Luigi Ferri – more specifically, over his leg.

"He's come down with the polio," the Death Sisters
announced to anyone who'd listen. "But keep it under
wraps. The family might not like everybody knowing."

And that was so. Grandmother Ferri was mortified
by the heavy hand of God that had landed on her little
Luigi's leg with too much force.

Her once robust and cherubic Luigi, a sensitive and
solicitous boy – always a good eater – had been
stricken. For weeks he hung between life and death.
And then, perhaps because he was so chunky, the
scales tipped in his favor. He lived.

But his leg was not sure about the decision. It, for
some reason, had decided on a very halfhearted course
of participation in the overall return to health.

It mutinied by withering just enough to cause poor
Luigi excruciating pain every time he tried to walk
normally. It did allow him to limp successfully – and

89

that initial, fervently wished-for blessing became, in time, a curse.

My grandmother, heartsick over her son's plight, resolved to do everything in her power to make Luigi feel good and to see himself as normal. And so did his doting sisters.

That is what they decided to do in the light. In the dark, however, they had an entirely different plan.

In the dark, they decided to make Luigi into a nice, useful eunuch with whom they could play forever and protect from every harsh aspect of life – or die trying. If they played their cards right, they'd have an adoring man at their constant beck and call, one who'd show them over and over again that they were the nicest women in the world.

To do this, they instinctively knew would be a little tough at first. But once they'd undone Luigi's feeble, boyish resistances, then it would be a cakewalk. He'd go into the permanent Little Brother Harem from which they'd summon him whenever he was needed. With a good tail wind, they'd fashion themselves a love slave better than a thousand husbands.

My grandmother got the ball rolling by sleeping near Luigi during his convalescence, and crying hysterically whenever he made any health-related gesture.

If he reached for water by himself, she'd cry and thank God out loud. If he swallowed it, she'd swoon and cross herself dramatically. If he smiled and joked, she'd repeat his words to everyone, petting each phrase as if it were scripture appearing in a rare, medieval bible.

When Luigi finally left his sickbed behind and began to go about on his own again, the sisters took over.

"I can't tell you're not walking normal," my mother would say four or five times a day.

"I'm going to Millillo's for some biscotti," Aunt Mary would decide, "and even though you could walk there as well as anybody else, I'll bring yours back for you. You just rest nice-nice and read, okay?"

One day, Ciara – kind to a fault – went so far that it backfired. A neighbor had brought Luigi a striped pullover, an impromptu present she thought he'd like – a Venetian gondolier shirt!

"Oh," said Ciara, taking the sweater and holding it away from its intended recipient. "Bella. Bella. But I don't know. Stripes seem so threatening. Luigi, darling, do these make you dizzy? Do they upset your stomach?"

Luigi, now a boy of twelve, burst into angry tears, grabbed the sweater, and threw it at Ciara.

"I don't want it," he cried. "Why not give it to a normal boy?"

Ciara, flabbergasted, began to tremble. She was wounded to the quick. When she related Luigi's passionate words to her mother and sisters, they all began sobbing.

"All our efforts cannot undue what has been done to poor Luigi," lamented my grandmother. "We'll just have to try harder."

By the time Luigi was twenty, he had never had a girlfriend, even though many girls found him to be quite an attractive fellow. (Through intense application, he'd become a prosperous accountant of some renown.)

"No one could stay married to me for long," he told his mother. "It's not fair for someone with my leg to marry a regular girl and make her miserable."

"Oh, no. So hard on yourself," my grandmother would cluck. "I'll tell you what. I'll let you go with Ciara and me to the market. And we'll buy all the stuff to make ricotta pie – your favorite – with the lemon zest. And we'll come home and make a nice one. Okay?"

"Okay," he said to his mother. "But your feet don't hurt do they? Your ankles aren't swollen again?"

"Pfffff," she said with the martyred resignation practiced by Italian mothers for nine centuries. "They could do with a little rubbing. But don't concern yourself. Just knowing you're here makes them feel better."

❧ Ianine ❧

In which the town eccentric's early life by the sea is chronicled

When Ianine Vanacore was a child she lived on the seacoast of the Adriatic, in a wild and beautiful spot from which the mountains of Albania were perceptible. She grew up wandering along the water, listening to the ocean closely. Sometimes it would say yes, then turn around and say no. Sometimes it insisted on blue, sometimes it wanted white, sometimes it received starlight.

From it came all manner of fish, strange objects, creatures, moods, and intentions that Ianine felt were her siblings. Now and then it invited human beings out into its mysterious rooms and they never came back.

For this, Ianine forgave it, even when it took her father. Still she wandered the coast, interpreting the sea as if she were its priestess or a humble and admiring friend.

From her mother, whose isolation grew oppressive after her husband's death, Ianine picked up a kind of wild, inner restlessness, a spiritual claustrophobia. The only thing that made it bearable was being outside, near the water, or better yet, being able to bathe or swim in it.

Both mother and daughter developed a real mania for almost hourly contact with the sea. They needed to touch the water, even if they just went down to the

93

shore and dipped in their toes. Without the sea, they'd droop as if all life and energy were being drained from their thin bodies.

To be sure, this ancient and refreshing way of life couldn't last.

After Ianine's "sane" and well-meaning uncles arrived for a visit, the wanderings and bathings were abruptly halted.

Ianine and her mother were carted off to Casamassima, protesting loudly, to live with Ianine's old Aunt Amalia, her mother's dull sister.

Within six months Ianine's mother packed up a few little toiletries, a book of Homer's poems, and ran away. She'd gone to the sea – onto it or into it – Ianine felt sure. And again, Ianine wasn't unforgiving: She expected that in any moment her mother would return and they'd both resume their former lives as acolyte mermaids.

But it didn't happen.

Ianine grew up without her sea, without her mother, and instead with Aunt Amalia's tutorials on religion and on the botanical, curative arts.

Ianine found that while her aunt had a very systematic and deliberate approach to the healing plants, her own was a different way. Much like how the sea had established its voice in her, so now did the plants. She struck out on her own with combinations and methods that at first alarmed her aunt.

But then, to the old lady's surprise, a lot of Ianine's strange concoctions worked. She had, for instance, made a funny smelling paste out of wormwood and other ingredients that could melt warts off with splendid results.

Amalia had to admit it: Ianine was hearing something important from the plants. The two began to work more as co-equals, and Ianine's reputation began to spread. People frequently came to consult her when traditional doctoring had failed, or in addition to it, or as a complete alternative.

Ianine, it was noticed with suspicion (which ultimately added to her mystique and success), spoke not so much in prose but more in poetry – confident, poetic streams. She didn't sound normal; that was for certain.

She didn't like to look people in the eye, but gazed more indirectly when giving instructions.

She washed a lot after any contact with those she treated.

And she'd ripple her body like a horse quivering to free himself of pesky flies on a hot day.

"The bugs are after me again," she'd exclaim, twitching like an electric eel. "No matter what I do or how much I wash, they simply will not let me be."

✎ "The Lawyer Who's Not Called For ✎ Is Paid with a Kick in The Pants"

In which Ianine's prowess with botanical herbs is debated

"She has to twitch like that," said my Aunt Ciara sympathetically. "She gets other peoples' diseases off her like that. Otherwise, they might stick to her when she's trying to cure them."

Aunt Ciara, as might be surmised, loved and championed Ianine. She felt she understood her perfectly and ran interference for her with skeptical people like my father.

"Sure, sure," my father would say. "You stick up for her, Ciara. You're just strange, whereas she's completely mad. I'd stick up for her, too, if I were you. She makes you look good!"

Then Ciara would laugh and my mother would yell at my father for teasing her sister too harshly.

"Leave Ciara alone. She's a saner person than you'll ever be."

"Maybe," said my father, "but she sure doesn't sound like it, always touting up that Ianine Vanacore. Did you hear that old buggy witch has lived on nothing but wine for the last three years?"

"She has to," Ciara countered. "She has something wrong with her stomach, poor soul."

"Hmmmph! Poor soul's got something wrong with her head. Poor soul's got something wrong with her

97

poor soul, more to the point. It's a disease of soul, if you want my opinion."

"Nobody wants it," flashed my mother. "A lawyer who's not called for is paid with a kick in the pants. So just shut up, will you? Ianine Vanacore's had a tough life, a lonely life, and God's compensated her with her calling. She's been blessed, not that you would know a blessed person if one bit you on your butt."

"Hmmmph," my father scoffed back. "I supposed that's another proof of someone's blessed state to you. They bite sane people on their posteriors. Just listen to the crazy, dirty way you're talking now, Palma. It makes me wince, the indelicacy of it."

"Oh, God," said my mother, now dripping with sarcasm, "please forgive me for offending You and my delicate violet of a husband who thinks he can shit on the good name of Ianine Vanacore, one of Your Saints Elect, and not expect to be called on it."

"Foul, foulmouthed woman!" cried my father, outraged. "I now understand why Socrates drank the hemlock. He drank it to escape his scourge of a wife. That was why, to get away from Xantippe. He couldn't have cared less about preserving the efficacy of the laws. He just wanted to have peace. Death, where is thy sting? When will I escape this hell?"

"Hey, there's the door!" My mother pointed dramatically. "You can leave any time and go find Zanstippy or whoever the hell you're so worried about. If you worried less about these dead fools you're always coming up with, and more about day-to-day business, we'd all get farther!"

"Ignorant, ignorant!" screamed my father, now choking with rage and tearing at his hair. "You have the erudition of a goat! Ignorant! Ignorant!"

"*I'm* ignorant? I'll tell you who's ignorant. Don't ever expect me to stand here while you mean-mouth Ianine Vanacore. I don't ever care to hear she's crazy out of your *ignorant* mouth again!"

My mother continued in lather. "She cured Luigi. She cured him of polio, do you hear me? The regular doctors didn't even give him a chance in hell. They didn't even want to look at him, scared bunch of bastards.

"But Ianine came, and from the moment my mother saw her, she had hope. And it was Ianine who saved him!

"She saved my little brother from death!" screamed my mother at full pitch, absolutely at one with her fury.

My father didn't believe it, but he shut up. Even though he was so mad he could hardly breathe, he pulled himself away from the brink of disaster.

As usual, my mother's beliefs were beyond logic, beyond anything he could ever muster up. For now at least, she'd put Ianine Vanacore in a shrine – and he wasn't going to be able to yank her out of it.

If he waited awhile, however, something would change. Ianine would cross one of the invisible wires my mother unconsciously spun to trip people up. Eventually even Ianine, with feet that so nimbly moved over land and sea, would stumble across my mother's spidery filaments.

Then, thought my father with some satisfaction, Ianine Vanacore would really have something to twitch about.

✎ Pasquale and the Stinging Nettles ✎

In which Aunt Ciara introduces me to Ianine Vanacore for medicinal and other reasons

One afternoon, on a particularly overcast and balmy Wednesday in Casamassima, my own chance to meet the mysterious Ianine Vanacore arose quite suddenly.

Aunt Ciara and I had been out picking greens for salad when I'd clumsily stumbled and fell headlong into a nasty patch of stinging nettles. Funny, I'd never noticed them before, there in the bed of foxglove. Within a half hour, my left eye had swollen shut with not so much as a narrow slit to see through. In its turn, my whole face began to swell and expand with alarming rapidity.

"Oh, oh, oh!" exclaimed Ciara. "We had better just drop everything and go see Ianine. She's right up the road here. Your eye looks terrible, Pasquale. Worse by the second."

"I don't know," I began hedging immediately. "Maybe it will clear up pretty soon."

"Oh, I see!" said Ciara. "Don't be afraid of Ianine. Ianine is no one you need fear. Trust me, Pasquale. She isn't."

With Aunt Ciara leading me along the road like a faithful guide dog, we made our way to Ianine's dilapidated house. Before we were to the threshold of the door, Ianine came energetically popping from the house like a skinny, black fox flowing out of its den.

She stood there, staring a little past me, yet I could tell she was taking everything in. Her hair, black and white streaks of energy, haloed her head. How old she was, was impossible to gauge. Also, though no one ever mentioned it, she had strong, white perfect teeth, which now flashed a beautiful smile at my Aunt Ciara.

"It's Ciara Ferri Manzari and the girl who sees it all from her right eye," she said. "Come here, girl. Stand here."

I went to her, though I didn't want to – unable to let Ciara down in anything, no matter how much it cost me.

"Stinging nettles want lady's slipper like the land wants the sea. And that's what we'll give them."

And with that, she went back into the house for a few minutes and reappeared with a little paper cone of moist plant matter.

"Go ahead, rub it on your face, girl," she instructed, looking up at the clouds and seemingly following them across the sky.

It was just a guess, but Ianine seemed like she was in a good mood. Whether it was because Ciara was there and she liked her or because of nothing in particular, Ianine appeared to be playful, wickedly so.

"Girl," she asked me, "what do you call the place where the sky and the land meet?"

"Well, a good place, I guess."

"Yes," she said excitedly, and for a terrifying second looked right at me. "That's true. But it's got a name. What is it?"

"I don't know – what?"

"Poetry," she said and clapped her hands gleefully. "It's poetry. You know, your Aunt Ciara said you like to write poetry."

"Oh, I do!" I said histrionically. "And if God grants me sight after this cursed day, I'll write it again."

"My mother wrote poetry," asserted Ianine, "with one foot in the water world and one foot in the land world."

I nodded my head earnestly in response. What she said seemed reasonable to me.

"She understands what you mean, Ianine," Aunt Ciara said.

"Oh?" said Ianine as she pivoted a little on one foot, swaying.

"Ianine Vanacore!" Suddenly a man's stern voice from inside the house came booming out to where we were standing. "Come in here. Come here!"

Immediately the lightness of the mood shifted and Ianine's famous quiver went through her limbs.

"No charge," she barked, rather kindly. "No charge for Ciara Ferri Manzari and little Cyclops. Your eye will be better, but go on. Go on, now."

She waved us off and went somewhat heavily back inside.

"Who's that man she's got in there?" I asked my Aunt Ciara. "Who is he that gets her so nervous?"

"Oh, it's no man at all," said my aunt, grimly. "It's her Aunt Amalia. That's *her* voice you heard."

"But I thought she was dead," I said incredulously.

"Well," said Ciara with a strange, muffled look. "It's not out of the question."

❧ The Opera Singer ❧

In which Grandmother Catto's famous cousin visits briefly and inadvertently creates class warfare

One day my father received a letter from his mother in Treviso. She was taking a moment to inform him that their young cousin, the famous opera singer, was home from touring the United States. It would be wonderful if she could stop by in Casamassima after an engagement in Naples and visit him and his family.

Thrilled to have "a visitor from civilization," my father agreed. He broke the good news to my mother, who huffed and puffed and resented the inconvenience. What to serve this woman? What to wear to greet her? How to know when she'd arrive? What to say to somebody who didn't work, but just flounced around the world dressing up like fake people from old stories and singing?

This was out of her league entirely. And she dreaded being upstaged by this stranger for whom she'd have to go way out of her way. What would be in it for her except lots of extra work? How would she keep up with her business?

And my father was no help. He hadn't even been able to pin down the exact day of his cousin's arrival, which meant my mother would have to be on her best behavior with an immaculate house and perfect food for three days running – a gruesome strain.

The more my father pulled out all his treasured pictures of Cugina Amelita and spread them around the parlor to bask in their glory, the more furious my mother became.

Here was Amelita as Carmen with spit curls, a mantilla, and a flamenco dress. Here she was as Violetta in *La Traviata*, looking consumptive and self-sacrificing. Here she was in the mad scene from *Lucia Di Lammermoor*, with a big bejeweled dagger and long, wild fright-hair.

"What's she got on in that scene, a nightgown?" jeered my mother as she'd pass by, cleaning like a Fury.

"No," said my father indignantly. "It's not a nightgown. It's the costume of a Druid priestess. She's Norma, the tragic Norma!"

"*Meraviglioso*, Norma the tragic Norma," my mother echoed my father with blatantly false enthusiasm.

"Palma," my father said, "your mother, all your sisters, even your father – the most spiteful man who ever drew breath – like opera. Why not you? What happened to you?"

"Focaccia." She spit out the word. "Focaccia happened to me. Ever notice where all my free time is spent? I don't have any. I don't get to see curtains come up. I get to see dough rise!"

My father decided to ignore this last remark, considering it was getting harder as the years passed for him to defend his nonworking status. He turned back to his photographs of Amelita and some of the many letters, articles, and souvenirs his mother had sent him chronicling his illustrious cousin's career. He'd collected these for a long time.

My mother, feeling ornery, sashayed over and picked one up at random and began reading.

"'...Of course it has shaken Amelita to the very marrow of her bones to have to proceed with this divorce – you know how religious she is. And having to get it in America like that has made her feel disloyal to Italy, on top of it' –

"What is this?" my mother asked. "Your mother wrote and told you Amelita got divorced! This is three years old. You never said a thing about it to me. And isn't that nice! Here I am breaking my neck cleaning this house for some high tragic priestess of DIVORCE? And who's she bringing with her? I thought she was bringing her husband. But which one is it? The first...the second...the *fifteenth*? No wonder she wears nightgowns so much!"

"That's enough of that!" warned my father.

"It certainly is," my mother said with disgust.

"She's not welcome in my house. Thus, I stop cleaning for high-class prostitutes."

Whack! She threw down her sopping wet cleaning rag and walked from the house.

After a few hours of "ethics" discussion with her older sisters and Uncle Franco, my mother felt as though she was not just being cantankerous in wanting to avoid the gay divorcée. My father's deceit was purposeful – definitely. He had wanted to hide the awful truth from his wife, knowing full well the consequences of his revelation.

My mother could forgive a lot of things – although not many spring to mind – but one thing she'd never forgive was the *moral "sophistication" of the elite.*

People who gave themselves privileges because they were rich or had status were the red flag to her bull. And she was, after all, a true Taurus and a democrat.

Why should Amelita be able to get a divorce whenever she wished, and remain respectable, still be fêted? Just because she could wear a nightgown and screech a little?

It wasn't going to hold water with Palma Ferri – and she returned home four hours after storming from the house to tell my father so, again and definitively. (As if he'd missed the point.)

But when she stormed back in armed with her family's coerced moral support, she was greeted by a deflating surprise: There sat my father, utterly crumpled and crestfallen, still surrounded by his Amelita memorabilia. And now there was a new letter on the pile, one that the postman had just delivered. It lay, unloved and halfheartedly thrown on top of its predecessors.

"You needn't worry about Amelita," mumbled my father with hardly any strength in his depressed voice. "She's decided not to come. She'd have to rush back to Naples so fast for her next engagement that it's not worth a visit to Casamassima!"

"Son of a bitch," stomped my mother. "I suppose we're not good enough for her to visit. Who the hell does she think she is?"

❧ Uncle Luigi's Famous Letter ❧

In which my father exhorts me to embrace art and not repeat the mistakes of his youth

As my father lackadaisically stuffed his revered scraps of Amelita's triumphs back into their folders, he came across another bit of family history – this one less illustrious but far more personal. Of all things to come floating back to consciousness at this time! Yet there it was: Uncle Luigi's nasty letter threatening him to stop courting Palma – or else.

Who had my father been when he received that letter so many millions of years ago? Who was he now? He read with fascination, a spectator to the phenomenon of his own past life:

Caro Signore Catto,

It has come to my attention through various reliable sources that my poor, unfortunate sister, Palmi Ferri, is being led by you down the primrose path to perdition. My respectable and honorable brothers, Stephano and Rocco, have given me their word that on two occasions they have come to the *pensione* where you are holed up, to beat you soundly on her behalf, but that both times you escaped your just desserts when Signora Aldonucci came downstairs and told them to go home or she'd call in the authorities. Out of respect for her wishes they let you escape, coward that you are.

To this I say only – You must come out some-time, Signore Catto, and when you do, an old lady's skirts will no longer hide you too well. My brothers will be waiting and my father also (unless he's at work.) Some people work for a living, as you may be unaware.

If I could only shed the unfortunate chains which bind my legs through a God-given illness visited upon me in early youth, I, too, would be chasing you through the streets, catching and throttling you with abandon, and leaving you half-dead like the slimy cur you are, your brains running out like translucent tomatoes squashed and oozing. (As you see, my thoughts are strong in proportion to my weak legs.)

If you do not desist at once from taking the evening passiagiata with my sister and speaking to her of frivolous matters such as marriage, there will be more trouble than you have days to live through.

Am I making myself perfectly clear, Joker?

Perhaps in your lustful and unwholesome heart there is one bit of kindness or charity left, and I suggest you listen to that and realize the truth. Palma is too good for you and she doesn't love you. She is merely in "the grip of a fleeting infatuation." Apparently you read her poems out of Dante and the like which have turned her better judgment over – but we who are not susceptible to such romantic tripe know the real tenor of the situation.

Why don't you go to church if you really care anything at all for my sister and confess your sins? Then get on with your life and leave my decent family alone. How long do you really think a quality girl such as my sister will be entertained by you reading her cute little poems about hell? And when that fascination wears off, what will be left? Absolutely nothing. Am I wrong?

Think about it and get out of our lives while you can. Let us part as friends while there is still time. Why shed blood over a ridiculous thing like marrying someone who doesn't want you? Stick to your profession, whatever it is, or get a fulfilling hobby instead.

Sincerely but with firm, unshakeable resolve, the resolve of a brother who loves his sister,

Luigi Ferri

Dazed and more depressed than usual, my father let Uncle Luigi's letter slip from his fingers to the floor. He covered his eyes with his forearm and sighed deeply, a Hamlet-like sigh.

"Cute little poems about hell!" my father said to me blankly as I went by.

"What?"

"That's how your brilliant Uncle Luigi, the cosmic accountant, described Dante's immortal masterpiece *The Inferno*. 'Cute little poems about hell.' Have you read that work, Pasquale?"

"Yes, I did."

"Are the poems cute, Pasquale? Are they cute, would you say?"

"No, they are not cute."

"That is right, Pasquale. They are not cute. And a person who says they are cute is an ax-murderer of the spirit. Why? Because words are deeds – and words used incorrectly are evil deeds, sins, abominations. Do you know what Buddhists are, Pasquale?"

"Yes, I do."

"Good girl. Well, their tradition says outright that words are deeds. They know something, the Buddhists. Do you know what they know in Casamassima, Pasquale? In this family specifically? About the power of the right word? About the spiritual power of THE WORD?"

"What?"

"Nothing. They know nothing. Pasquale, are you writing your poems and stories, still?"

"Yes!"

"Everyday?"

"Yes."

"Good, Pasquale, good. Will you promise me something, I who am merely the animated corpse called your father?"

"Well, maybe if you tell me what it —"

"No, no, Pasquale. No. Just promise this one thing, okay?"

"Okay."

"Promise me you'll stick to poems and stories and take love with a big grain of salt, Pasquale. Promise me you'll have the life I never had, the one I was too weak to claim."

"Oh, dear…"

"No, No, Pasquale. This is very important. I am not trying to be self-indulgent. I'm trying to save you from the ax-murderers of the spirit."

"I appreciate it…"

"No. No you don't, Pasquale. I can tell you don't. Listen, will you?"

"I'm listening."

"Okay. See, Love was here before human beings were. It's older and stronger – and it's completely blind to the individual. Do you understand? It's a plot looking for characters. See?"

"No."

"All right. I'll try it this way. You've read how they say Love is a god or goddess – strong, powerful?"

"Sure."

"Okay, well, that's not metaphor. That's literally so. Love's an independent animated force – and once It gets you, It'll toss your life around and entertain Itself at your expense. You need to be really strong, you see? Because in time, It will dissipate, but you'll still be there, see?"

"Not exactly."

"Okay, Pasquale. One more time. Romantic love lands people in preposterous, narrow cages. And sometimes they don't find the keys – and they rot in the goddamn cage. See now?

"Look for a minute at how you feel when somebody says Dante's poems are cute – you're instantly defensive, right? Tired, furious, displaced. Why? Because you're in the grip of the reductive, the inane.

"And Pasquale, people who aren't inane and reductive can't be with ones who are – or they'll get sick and die. I'm telling you, Pasquale, if you betray your creative life you could end up like that – doing time, Pasquale, in the prison of the inane and reductive.

"And that's not what I want for you. I want you to be more like Cugina Amelita. She writes her own ticket in this world. She comes and goes as she pleases and has fewer cages than most people, you see? That's why your mother hates her so much – because Amelita, she's a creator. See? She has real freedom."

"That, I see," I told my father, looking him straight in the eye with Athena-like intensity. "That I've seen for a long, long time."

"Good!" exclaimed my father, rising from his chair with a burst of energy. "Good, Pasquale. Now we're getting somewhere, finally. Well spoken. Good.

"I'll leave you with this one last thought for today, and then I'm not going to worry about you anymore for at least two weeks. Are you listening?"

"Yes."

"Okay. Here it is. 'The most dangerous threat to the child is the unlived life of the parents.' Think about that, Pasquale, okay?"

"Okay!"

"Okay. Run off now and write more or something. I need my nap after all this, Pasquale. My nice, long nap."

il arazzo

❧ Stephano e Rocco ❧

In which my uncles expertly hold forth on the idiotic

Somehow, discussions with my father, ever since I'd taken my Shutter Vow, seemed to do me real good. True, he wasn't going to work out of his own depression, but he at least knew he should've. And I knew, too, that he wanted to inspire me out of any future malaise I might be approaching. Maybe he was a good father, I decided charitably. Maybe he was the best father I could hope for with my temperament. Or did I feel that way simply *because* I'd inherited *his* temperament, and all his flaws felt natural? How to know?

It began to get confusing again, cause and effect stuff, so I abandoned it a little and went over to visit my uncles Stephano and Rocco. They were always good for comic relief, and experiencing the contrast between them and my father was better than electroshock therapy.

When I got to my grandparents' home, the family home where Luigi, Stephano, and Rocco all still lived (unmarried, though well into their late thirties), there were no surprises waiting.

Stephano and Rocco were sitting in the kitchen, waiting for the cool of the day when they'd both lope down to the piazza for the evening stroll. The evening stroll was a good time to look at women and at peoples' clothes, and nose around and pretend they were seeking business opportunities. They did it every day of their lives, and if they'd keeled over dead, their bodies would've gone down and done it without them. It was not a conscious process anymore.

On this particular afternoon Stephano and Rocco were discussing their favorite topic, "So-and-So Is An Idiot." It went something like this:

Rocco: "Do you know Aldo Millillo?"

Stephano: "Yeah, sure."

Rocco: "He's an idiot."

Stephano: "So's his brother Fredo."

Rocco: "Oh, yeah. A real idiot. No lie."

Stephano: "It's a toss-up as to which one of them brothers is the bigger idiot, if you'd ask me."

Rocco: "Aldo seems like a bigger idiot to me. But I don't know Fredo as well. So I can't really say. Hi, Pasquale. How you doing?"

Stephano: "Hi, Pasquale. No, it's a toss-up. They're both really, really idiots."

Rocco: "No kidding! You know who else is an idiot? I didn't realize 'til the other day when I ran into him for a few minutes —"

Stephano: "Who?"

Rocco: "LoLo Lagravanese. Now that guy's a real bona fide idiot."

Stephano: "Jesus. You've got that down."

Rocco: "No, am I right?"

Stephano: "Oh, you're right. LoLo Lagravanese isn't probably even sharp enough to be an idiot. He's what you call a sub-idiot."

Rocco: (laughing) "A sub-idiot. I'll go for that. He's a sub-idiot."

Stephano: "Yep, a sub-idiot."

Rocco: "That's rich. A sub-idiot. *Rich!*"

Stephano: "A sub-idiot. One hundred percent."

Rocco: "One hundred percent? That much credit you're giving him?"

Stephano: "Yeah, I'm treating him like a king, here."

Rocco: "Wait, wait. I just thought of somebody who really *is* an idiot."

Stephano: "Who?"

Rocco: "Turo Mancuso."

Stephano: (all crazy) "Oh my God! Oh my God! Turo Mancuso is the biggest idiot who ever idioted! Oh, my God!"

Pasquale: "Well, I gotta go now."

Stephano: "Ciao. Ciao, Pasquale. Be a good girl."

Rocco: "Yeah, Pasquale, don't be an idiot."

Stephano: "Ha ha ha ha ha. 'Don't be an idiot,' he says. Ha ha ha ha ha."

Stephano and Rocco also had a routine called "So-and-So Is An Honest-To-God Bitch," but they rarely did it in front of me. I had to be lucky enough to overhear it by accident. Even then, it had changed over the years and had gotten somewhat tamer than its original form. This, my mother told me, was due to her deft editing technique of hitting Rocco in the teeth one day when her name had been selected from their hopper of eligible honest-to-God bitches. She hadn't gone for that honor one bit.

Another routine, once a stalwart favorite of theirs, had been "I'd Rather Be Dead Than Work For So-and-So." That one had to be abandoned because Grandpa Ferri had offered to castrate both "boys" if he ever heard them refuse to work for anybody *ever*. This offer had its intended effect, and even though they briefly considered changing their format to "I'd Rather Be A Sorry-Ass Eunuch Than Work For So-and-So," it just never had the appeal of their initial enterprise. My uncles, I came to appreciate, were traditionalists, classicists, and very resistant to even minor changes in form.

❧ Christmas Eve Crisis ❧

In which calamari become a raison d'etre and a suitable symbol of Jesus

In Casamassima, by the time Christmas Eve rolled around, it never mattered if Stephano and Rocco had successfully enumerated every idiot in their environ, or if my mother's focaccia had put more lucre in her bank account, or if Aunt Pig had made it out of Purgatory, or if Bibi and Costanzo ate all their fig pastries and ceased mourning. It didn't matter if Saracens, Romans, Bourbons or mummified Sicilians ran the government.

When Christmas came to Casamassima, it was a very stabilizing event, perhaps because every person there knew what he or she would be doing, whether they wanted to or not. Any certainty in life was, after all, a comfort of some sort, the world being so unstable and wild.

The itinerary of events included a meatless evening meal of calamari simmered in tomato sauce with finely chopped onion and basil, a promenade to Mass, then a promenade home to wait for the stroke of midnight when the figure of Baby Jesus would be placed in His crib in the miniature manger scene. Any family with two sticks to rub together owned such a presipio, the more detailed and expensive, the better. If you didn't have one, sorry, you had to go look at the one in church.

In the Ferri family, it was Uncle Franco who manned the manger scene, overseeing its careful unpacking, the assembly of its background (a kind of ruined Roman temple with lots of tiers, nooks, crannies, and mossy terraces) and most importantly, the placement of the many figures.

Each year Franco took "Christmas Eve Day" off and traded in the lucrative cutting of hair for unpaid presipio management. This he did religiously (pun intended) with artistic relish. The whole day went to it and the whole family wandered in and out to check his progress. He could've done without some early critical input, but that was not the way life went.

"Hey, Franco, that elephant looks ratty," my mother said. "It looks like some grey dough with a tube stuck in it. Can't we have a better elephant?"

"No kidding," chimed in Uncle Rocco. "That elephant looks like an idiot!"

"Palma, I ordered a new one. It didn't come. What can I say?"

"You can say, 'I love him even if he's ratty,'" said little Gina, who was loyal to the elephant and resistant to any change in the presipio.

"I'm going for a long walk," glowered my grandfather. "I may come back to this house or I may not!"

"And the Wise Men," persisted my mother, "I can't find the fourth one."

"There are only three," said my father. "Everybody knows that."

"That's not how I remember it," she said.

"Hey, hey, don't start. Here, Palma," Uncle Franco calmed my mother, "here's the fourth one, okay?" He picked up a shepherd with better than average clothes and showed her.

"Sure, there it is," she agreed, shooting my father the I-know-religion-and-you're-a-stinking-heathen look.

"Ahhhh, Jesus," said my father, covering his eyes and shaking his head in disgust.

"Yes, where *is* Baby Jesus?" asked Gina anxiously. "Don't you pack him on top usually? He's not here anywhere and everybody's been put out now!"

It was true. There in the splendid ruins milled kindly donkeys, sumptuously clad camels, solicitous sheep, pacific oxen, fresh faced shepherds, angels (both archangels *and* seraphim) and of course, Mary and Joseph staring at an empty manger – which now seemed in danger of remaining empty! All Christmas!

"What!" Franco began panicking. "Isn't there a little linen bundle here? I put Him in a little linen bundle last year when I packed. Ciara, Ciara, come out here!"

When Uncle Franco called Aunt Ciara from her kitchen duties, she came running, braid flying. She'd been cleaning the calamari, and tiny purple-black stains were dappling her fingers.

"What? What?" she asked, reacting to Franco's panic.

"Jesus! He's gone!"

"God is dead!" said my father very seriously to befuddle Ciara and whip up the spectacle he saw forming before him. Now there'd be some fun. The Ferri histrionics did have some charm for him.

"What?" Ciara looked shocked.

"Jesus is missing."

"That's a bad sign," my grandmother came hobbling in on her aching feet to tell everyone. "I knew that the first year without Aunt Pig would be bad. We can't even go get the straw out of her bed to put in the manger scene this year! If no one else thinks of her, I do!" She began to cry.

"Mama, stop with Aunt Pig for right now," comforted Ciara. "Let's try and find Jesus."

"Yes, it's too bad you don't have Aunt Pig anymore, especially now that you lost Jesus," reasoned my father, setting up his in-laws. "You could've got her over here and stuck HER in the manger – she looked like both Jesus *and* the animals gazing at Him at the same time."

"OH MY GOD!" my mother screamed. "You have no feelings for anyone, if you can say that! You are *sfacciato*!"

"What did he say?" my grandmother asked. She hadn't heard through her snuffling.

"He says he misses Aunt Pig at Christmas, too," said Ciara with a merciful translation.

"Oh, what's wrong with that? That's nice. A nice son-in-law I've got."

After a day-and-a-half hunt through every wrapping and box available, no figure of Jesus was resurrected. Another mystery was upon the family – and too late to buy or borrow a baby deity. People were selfishly hanging onto them at this time of year.

"Oh, we should really get an extra couple little Jesuses for next year – to avoid this," planned Aunt Mary.

"We'll make one," said Ciara. "We'll make one out of dough and use calamari bone for the translucent halo! He'll be just as nice."

"Oh Ciara," Franco was skeptical. "Do you truly believe you can make one? Is that kind of sacrilegious or something?"

"No," said my father. "Let her make Jesus out of an octopus if she's got a mind to. Jesus is symbolized by a fish, right? And an octopus is close!"

"Don't believe anything that comes from his mouth," my mother warned.

Ciara knew she could do it. So she just went in the kitchen and did it, baked up a reasonably accurate baby figure with a halo of milky smoothness.

On Christmas Eve she brought it forth.

"It looks better than that elephant," muttered my mother as she handed it to Gina who placed the Infant Christ in his crib on the stroke of midnight, grandly ushering Christmas into the family parlor.

❧ Palio del Viccio and the ❧ Festival of St. Nicholas

In which two Feast days reveal cultural identity and the resultant joys

Besides Christmas, there were a few other major celebrations without which my family could and would not do. With the exception of my father and grandfather, everyone waited with bated breath for February 16th and May 8th.

On these two glorious days, we went into Bari, the larger adjoining city, for two amazing Pugliese festivals. The one in February was called Palio del Viccio and mainly consisted of ten guys on horses trying to tilt at a water bag hung high up on a pole. Whoever hit it and broke the bag got the *viccio* – the turkey!

This particular festival had enormous appeal for Rocco and Stephano, who had once *almost* managed to rent a horse for a few months before the contest and had *almost* gotten to practice tilting at an old flour sack filled with wet leaves.

Though they'd never done either of these two things, they talked about the particular challenges and nuances of the "sport" as though they'd been brought up in a kind of Olympic village training camp for water-bag breaking, and had won about four thousand turkeys in the course of their stellar careers.

The real fun of this festival was hearing them criticize every movement made by the ten supple and extremely graceful young men who were actually competing.

Every year there came the moment when my mother, having taken all she could of her brothers' carping braggadocio, would turn to them ritualistically in the middle of the crazy, cheering crowd and yell at the top of her voice:

"Shut up, already! I've had it with you. You couldn't win a goddamn turkey if the only water bag you had to hit was under your asses in a chair, and all you had to do was sit down hard. You'd miss it, you understand what I'm saying? You'd miss it."

"No, we wouldn't!" Stephano would yell back, oblivious to how ridiculous his retort made him seem.

"Oh yes, yes you would!" my mother would scream in turn.

"No, I don't think we would," Rocco would add, furthering the ludicrousness of it all.

Whatever they said, however, was just great. The crowded day with its swirling color, food, music, its chivalric echoes of a medieval past, and the gorgeous bodies of the men and horses never failed to please our hearts' thirst for edifying spectacle.

Standing there in the crowd, clutching my beloved Aunt Ciara's hand on one side and my sweet Aunt Mary's on the other, I felt connected to my own life, the life of my people, and to our place on the planet for a thousand years running, backwards and forwards.

If anyone had asked me or would ever ask me, "What does it feel like to be perfect?" I'd have told them, "It feels like this. To stand with your own on a day like this, in this place, and want nothing more. It feels like Jesus kissing you full on the lips. It feels like winning the turkey in the jousting contest of life, and claiming that delicious bright-feathered prize."

Our full-blown enthusiasm for Palio del Viccio, considerable as it was, was rivaled by our attachment to the Feast of Saint Nicholas.

Whereas the turkey-joust festival spilled over with secular joie de vivre and lots of vicarious competitive energy, the Feast of St. Nicholas offered a calmer, lovelier spectacle, verging on the sacred, promising affiliation with the sacred – but not quite fulfilling that promise. It still had its free-for-all character.

The Feast of St. Nicholas harkened back to the eleventh century when sixty-two Christian sailors, unduly attached to the saint who would later become "Santa Claus," stole his holy bones from the heathen Muslims and sailed with their desiccated prize for Bari, Christian Bari!

"That would have been one trip to pass up," my mother would comment every year. "Imagine having to smell somebody's bones all the way from Turkey! No thanks!"

"They would've had the odor of jasmine and roses," reported Aunt Ciara, "The fragrance of immortality, Palma. Because they were saints' bones, understand?"

My mother took it in out of deference to what she believed to be her sister's closeness to God. But basically, she was skeptical. To her, bones were bones.

"Well, more power to them if they had the stomach for it; at least we get to have this festival. I should be home working, but let's just say this is a great day and enjoy it!"

"Okay," everyone agreed. But it was never that easy. Away from her daily servitude to focaccia, my mother swung mood-wise between giddy hilarity and crippling guilt. By far, her wisecracking was the more interesting pole.

This year, as she watched the caravel on wheels carrying the antique statue of St. Nicholas through the streets to the Basilica of San Nicola, she was in rare form. Nothing escaped her scrutiny, as the oompah band leading the procession solemnly played the Italian national anthem.

Two of the standard bearers, just in front of the Saint himself, leapt into my mother's focus. How she could see so well and so far from our spot on the porch of San Nicola's Basilica was beyond me. But she could.

"Madonna mia! Look who they got carrying the flags this year," she said incredulously. "It's the DiCenzo twins. Look, Pasquale, they're just your age and they're the size of cows already. Can you believe it?"

"Oh, come on," said Aunt Mary, peering down to the street. "They look kind of cute. Those standards are heavy. They've got a big job, those poor kids."

"Hey, they're up to it," my mother confirmed. "It looks like their mother's been feeding them lard to get 'em ready. And she put them in pink on top of it. Pink tulle. Disgraceful. Pasquale, do you see how bad pink makes you look if you're fat?"

"So what SHOULD they be wearing?" I asked, all snotty.

"Some bags over their heads," said Uncle Stephano.

"Bags over their heads," Rocco jumped in to admire his brother's rapier wit. "Ha ha ha. That's *rich*."

"God, why didn't I stay home?" my mother queried the world which had betrayed her with its less-than-aesthetic elements. "To be subjected to this. What a miserable sight. I can't go anywhere. I'm cursed. Look at those twins, will you?"

Without meaning to make obvious fun of her sour sister's appetite for misery, my Aunt Mary started sniggering. Within seconds, Uncle Alfredo joined in, and pretty soon everybody was laughing.

Turning in repugnance from the puffing, sweating twins, my mother was greeted by the sight of her entire family guffawing. It took her, I could tell, quite by surprise.

For a moment she narrowed her left eye like she was getting ready to attack. But then, the corners of her red, shapely lips turned up – all the way up. And she began to laugh, too, at herself. She laughed and laughed.

"Quit it, you fools," she said, catching a breath here and there. "I'm going to have to pee if you keep it up. It's not funny. Keep it up and I'm not walking home with you. I mean it."

"Good," Ciara laughed on, "you stay here with St. Nicholas and the twins. We'll see you in Casamassima. Who needs you, Palma?"

So there stood my mother in the heart of the Festival of Saint Nicholas – at the end of the Via del Carmine, poised just so between the two stylized bulls that support its huge columns – laughing and trying hard not to pee.

I would be lying if I told you I didn't love her at that moment, in spite of every niggling, crotchety thing she'd ever done or would do again in five minutes, once she'd come to her senses.

But for right then, she was essentially beautiful, unguarded and free – free of her focaccia, free of my father's claims on her sense of duty, free of having to tend and shape my attitude and me. It must have felt good, I realized deeply. She was free in that moment, even of herself, a self from which she, most of all, wanted a vacation.

And wasn't that the purpose of a festival like that of St. Nicholas, the patron saint of children and sailors?

To feel free and expansive and playful, and like your very bones had set sail for somewhere that welcomed them as miraculous?

il fato

❧ L'America! ❧

In which Great-Uncle Giuseppe explains American culture

When Uncle Giuseppe sailed home from a three-year "visit" to the United States, my mother's family invited him over to eat and celebrate. After a two-hour meal that culminated with the famous lethal sponge cake, he began. Everyone was all ears and very excited. If it were a really favorable report they were going to hear – look out! Grandfather Ferri had begun to toy with emigrating, and that would be a serious proposition.

"First off," began Uncle Giuseppe, "I made a big mistake. I should've gone to Brazil with Gian-Carlo (his cousin), not to the United States."

"Why?" everyone asked.

"Well, because at least they understand the Latin soul – and they speak decently. In the United States, forget about it! English is a tough language.

"They've got a lot of strange misconceptions about Italians, too. Like, did you know that we are 'Africans?'"

"What?" everyone puzzled.

"Yes, we're black Africans there."

"But Africans are Africans and Italians are Italians, usually."

"Yeah, well, not there. They've decided that Italians have darker skin than 'Americans' and that means we're Africans. Greeks are Africans, too!"

"Well, why do they say that? And what about Americans who are Negroes? They are or are not Americans? Who *are* Americans?"

"Oh, yes. Good query, intelligent query. I'm not sure how to answer. I only know they – I mean the people in control of things – are always thinking about how to make sure 'Africans' – even if they're Italians – get the hardest jobs, the backbreakers!"

"Oh, that sounds terrible."

"Well, it is. It was. Also, they have communities where you're supposed to live, depending on who and what you are, how you believe, your color, and how much money you have – but they all say they did away with that in 1776. That's their history, they say. Democracy is their big thing."

"But, it's not true?"

"Well, maybe it is. I didn't see everywhere. It's just too big a place. I can't hold myself out as an expert. I mean some people there seem to be doing quite well for themselves. I can't complain, not with my luck. I oversaw the construction of twenty-three houses, mansions, really – for very, very rich people. They pay a lot if you can catch them in the right mood – needing stonework, masonry, tile – you know what I mean. I worked just north of New York City, in the country."

"So did you eat well there?"

"Certainly. I cooked my own food – else, forget it. They have, you might say, a very limited cuisine. And scared! They were terrified of macaroni, tomato sauce, calamari..."

"What! No! Are you joking?"

"Oh, I wish I were. But no kidding. If you offer average Americans a chance to have some breaded calamari, say, prepare yourself for resistance. They look at you like you're a cannibal! Don't even let on about liking snails."

"Oh dear," said my grandmother, who glanced down at the bedspread of crocheted medallions she was always making as though it would vanish from her busy fingers. Her sidelong glance at her husband assured her that he was taking everything her brother said with a measured credulity. But what would he ultimately decide? She couldn't get a read on his mood.

"Let me tell you another thing about America," Uncle Giuseppe continued. "It's a cultural desert – no *real* aesthetic holds them together – just making money and getting ahead as fast as possible. That's their 'glue' to life."

"There's nothing wrong with that," said my grandfather with grumpy defiance. "You've come home with a fat pocketbook, right?"

"Yes, but you know what you just said? You said I came home – and that's the thing. Here I know who I am. I can go down to the church, pull out the records – six hundred years worth of my family right there.

"In America, who am I?

"I'll tell you who I am. A big nobody who's being bossed around by people who are so isolated they think Africa's a country. And who live in fear of snails!

"What can you do with that? We're dealing here with a bunch of people who, even if they're rich, don't make important distinctions or think about what's exquisite to eat or wear or look at. You understand? They're too busy for the gorgeous detail. See what I mean?"

"Sure," said my grandfather. "You're saying you're sorry you can't get some leotards on and be in the ballet."

"What? What does that mean?" Uncle Giuseppe asked his brother-in-law incredulously. "Have I said an offensive thing?"

"Oh, how late it is," my grandmother marveled. "Anyone for a little more sponge cake? Giuseppe, what fun to have my little brother back home."

"Sure, sure, Vincenza. *Sorella mia*, how good to look at your sweet face." Giuseppe kissed his sister and everyone but my grandfather goodnight and left. He hadn't said nearly all he'd wanted to about America.

But my grandfather had heard enough! He decided then and there to send his eldest son, Raymond over to America to make a little money. Then, if that worked out, the whole family just might want to replicate Uncle Giuseppe's lucrative jaunt to the new world.

As a good student of horticulture, my grandfather wasn't terribly concerned with deracination. With a little attention, a little luck, things that were transplanted could do better than in their original soil. He didn't care, on that night at least, to consider that in some cases they died.

❧ Biscotti and Blue Fire ❧

In which our magic circles are besieged

"What, you're making a double batch?" my mother quizzed Aunt Mary as they busied themselves in my grandmother's kitchen. "Who you gonna feed, the DiCenzo twins?"

My mother, Aunt Mary, Ciara, my grandmother, and I were all gathered in the family homestead ("headquarters," as my father called it) to make biscotti. That, at least, is what my mother told me we were going there for on the short walk over. But it wasn't quite correct…and even I, who was not wired into their "sisterhood circuit board" knew that.

No, we were going over to talk about my grandfather's distracted angry silence, a mood he'd embraced fervently since Uncle Giuseppe's description of the United States. Something ominous had taken hold of him that night and as usual, he wasn't going to share his mind with anyone until he was good and goddamn ready – least of all with my grandmother. Why let *her* in on anything concerning their life together?

The silence around her husband, my grandmother explained, was becoming an unbearable presence, and it was pushing the whole family down, crushing it with the big unanswered question.

Making biscotti, my Aunt Mary decided, would help fill the void a little and it would be a nice time to talk things out. And the best biscotti for such a trying time would be the soft biscotti with sugar frosting and marmalade in the middle.

"Get me five cups of flour and eight teaspoons of baking powder. Right here, Palma. Yes, and the sugar – one cup. Right here. Put it all in this bowl. Nice, nice; I love this dolphin bowl, don't you, Palma? Hurry."

"Yes, yes, Mary. I'm coming. I suppose you think I forgot how to make biscotti."

"The thing of it is," my grandmother began from her seat at the kitchen table, "it's like a blue fire flaring all around him, all the time. Hey, those eggs are nice and fresh. I got four of them just for these biscotti. Anyway, the story, the old tale, is about how when magicians conjured up the Devil, they'd draw a chalk circle around themselves – hey, put a little more than two-thirds cup of milk, I don't like 'em dry – a conjuring circle to keep them safe, see? The Devil couldn't get in it –"

"Where the hell is the lard?" my mother demanded. "Pasquale, go in the cupboard and get it and put four tablespoons in here, now."

"But I'm listening to Grandma," I asserted.

"No, Pasquale," my grandmother said. "Go get the lard. Help your mother, Pasquale. God, you're getting so grownup. You're only about five years – is it only five years? – younger than Uncle Raymond. You know what he's doing now? In Bari?"

"What?" I asked, spooning the lard into Aunt Mary's now bulging bowl. "Grandma, what?"

My grandmother had grabbed the huge bowl to do the final mixing of ingredients herself. "He's shoeing donkeys for the army. Making pretty good money, not great, but all right. And he likes donkeys. Mary, use the rest of the lard to grease that pan. Not that one –

the other pan. So, the conjuring circle kept the magician safe – now in your grandfather's case, the Devil would put a circle around Himself to keep your grandfather out – Ciara! Ciara, what's the matter? *Ciarina mia*, hey!"

We all looked over to where Aunt Ciara was sitting silently at the table opposite my grandmother, in the chair my grandfather always used. She looked awfully small and doll-like – and very wistful.

"Oh, nothing. Agita maybe. Maybe nothing."

"What nothing?" my grandmother kept after her.

"Oh, I heard that Costanzo Fonticone is going to marry Lidia Tartaglia, that's all."

"WHAT!!" My mother dropped her mixing spoon with an audible clunk. "That Dirty Bag? That Dirty Bag who was after Cesare, Anna Posa's Cesare?"

"Yes, she's moving in right across the street. I saw her walking Bibi."

"No, no, no," everyone spit out in unison. Their minds leapt from Grandfather's horrid mood, a possible enforced emigration and the end of our collective happiness in the land of our forefathers and mothers, to something really important! Gossip! The biscotti dough – vanilla-colored and aromatic – was, for a while, yesterday's news.

Remembering it for a moment, however, they went back to it with intense looks and renewed vigor. Mary and my mother rolled the dough into fifty or so little balls, shoveled them into the oven. That done, they were free to *really* talk.

Aunt Ciara and I remained in the kitchen as the others went into the parlor chattering about the bomb Ciara had dropped. Costanzo, I had a feeling, was about to be raked over the coals. My mother was getting that bituminous look.

With everyone else gone, Ciara and I were now in charge of the ten-minute baking process. I searched my aunt's face and my suspicions were confirmed. Ciara was not in the slightest upset over Costanzo wedding Lidia, not a bit. It was something else. She'd said what she did in order to avoid telling.

"It's sitting in this chair," she explained. "Pasquale, something *real* bad's going to happen. The chair's picked it up and it told me. Oh, your poor Grandma, Pasquale. I've known for awhile, but this is a strong knowing."

"Aunt Ciara," I asked her, full of fear, "did the Crow Mother come to you in a dream?"

"No," said Ciara, "not this time. This time it was very strange. It was Benno. My Benno came back to see me – but it wasn't asleep-type dreaming. It was just-walking-up-the-street-in-broad-daylight dreaming. Don't you say anything, Pasquale. You won't, will you?"

"No, I never would."

"Good girl. There's nothing to do but keep living through each day and night now. Pasquale?"

"What?"

"Do you think if you were to go over to America that you'd be okay there? That you'd grow up good there?"

"Yeah, I would. If you come. Otherwise, I wouldn't."

"Well, you might get that wish."

When the biscotti were done, Ciara and I took them out, cooled them, cut each in half, and put orange marmalade in their middles. Then we frosted them with powdered sugar mixed in a little water, and served them to the other women. Ciara took the biggest, best-shaped one and gave it to my grandmother.

"Save some for Raymond," Grandmother reminded us. "He'll be home this weekend to tell us his donkey stories. And if you don't put some aside, Rocco and Stephano will eat them all."

❧ Raymond ❧

In which a railroad accident in New York changes the Family forever

Uncle Raymond at nineteen was the slender prince of all fairy tales, the young god of all myths. With his clear, grey-green eyes and wavy blonde hair, he would've looked quite at home lounging on the upper deck of a luxury liner, or snapping a towel in the row team's locker room of some American ivy league school.

He would've looked at home in such places, but it was his fortune to be born in Casamassima, a decidedly un-luxurious place. His compensation was a mother who welcomed her lastborn son as the absolute flower of perfection, and who believed in him as her reward for an otherwise hard and restricted existence.

One look at the two of them together, gazing at each other with amused and bemused satisfaction, told the whole tale. Whatever one did, the other found fascinating and worth mention. Theirs was a love affair which never outgrew its first few months' intensity; it went on and on with increasing involvement.

Raymond, a noticeably sweet-tempered person, had a distinct advantage in life, being the favored son of the mother. Whereas some people had to earn a glimpse into the various promised lands on earth, he'd been born into one and had never known a different place.

For all anyone could guess, Grandfather may have taken a secret and perverse delight in sending Raymond off to America, finally breaking up a twosome that excluded him quite naturally from its magic circle. Not that he wanted inclusion exactly, but he didn't like witnessing others' effortless joys.

When Raymond understood his father's will, he wasn't at all resistant. He wanted very much to sally forth and make his mark, and send for his mother or provide her with all manner of comfort. It was he who would lift her from poverty and crudity. He would be her savior.

He silenced her weeping and fear with lots of love and youthful bravado. In the end, she forced herself to admit that it was selfish not to champion his cause, even if it hadn't been his originally.

He wanted to go and have the continuing adventure of life, and how could she say no to such a strong, confident spirit? It was the spirit she'd prayed he would carry.

He left with his mother's tearful blessings. But underneath somehow, my grandmother felt like she was the bait her husband had used to lure her son away.

Somehow, something about his going wasn't quite right. Her uneasiness became a constant, nagging companion, one that the other children couldn't nudge over even for a few minutes. They realized, quite correctly, that their mother's soul was elsewhere. It was a stowaway in their brother's rucksack, the "big, woeful rucksack" he'd carried off on his hopeful young back.

Because of this, it came as absolutely no surprise to my grandmother that within six months of his landing in America, Uncle Raymond was dead, killed in a railroad accident near Ithaca, New York.

He'd been one of four men working the lever of a handcar when it had overturned, jumped the rail. The other three boys were thrown free without a scratch. But Uncle Raymond was pinned under the heavy car.

It had crushed his chest and back and burst his heart, and nothing could be done to help him. The other boys, one of them his cousin, held his hands and feet while he died.

My grandmother began to see the last sky he'd seen lying on his broken back in the tangled woods of upstate New York. It was, she said, white and blank, and the sun was overly bright. It was June, too hot, cruelly humid.

He couldn't be sent home, the initial letter said. They'd find a place for him in a rural cemetery with some Catholics in it. The Railroad would handle it. They'd find a suitable place, not to worry about that part.

His clothes were sent: two shirts, three undershirts, one pair of dress pants, and a jacket. (No shoes. He'd only had one pair.)

When they arrived, my grandmother held out her arms and received them with most tender respect. She reached into the pants' pockets and there were a few American coins in them – two dimes and an Indian-head penny.

She looked at the foreign coins for quite a while, placed them back in the pocket, then took the little bundle and put it in her old dowry trunk. She didn't cry for months, just became more silent and withdrawn. At first she'd just go sit by the trunk. Then, she began to open it and cry every day for many exhausting hours.

My grandfather got another letter, this one from an insurance company in New York; a check for close to two thousand dollars was in it. That was the going rate for handsome Italian boys.

It seemed a vast sum. Grandfather, in his turn, looked at the foreign "currency" for quite a while. He already knew what he was going to do with it.

His son had accomplished what he'd been sent to do, and this was the proof. That was the way to look at it. How else? Now he knew how it would go.

His loyal, protective children would come if he took their brokenhearted mother. They'd bring their spouses, children, whoever or whatever they needed to follow her.

They'd all go over and finish what had been started. The blood seed was already planted. Once there, Grandfather eventually would have the orchards he wanted, not work for elitist priests. They'd have big homes, businesses, respect, and comfort. In time, my grandmother would come around. Her grief would lift. She'd see the positive meaning of the sacrifice that was made.

In America, they'd start again – in New York where one of their own already had a little piece of land and a small stone marker that said FERRI in large letters.

✎ Le Nozze di Vincenza ✎

There, she's lifted off again.
 Up over the harbor, just
 dusting Liberty's torch
 a few tears sprinkled on Ellis
 and completely aloft above the Atlantic.
By morning, still dewy and floating
 she throws her shadow
 a flower dark shawl
 over Sardinia.

By lunch time
 to the tune of putti laughter
 she dances with Verdi (giddy with relief)
 in the Neapolitan sky.

Chagall, vacationing in Italy that very day
 saw her cloudlike above Bari
 and she inspired all such paintings he ever did

 of floating dancing lovers
 over the villages of Europe

 swirling petals
 light as arias
 violin-hearted
 mermaid betailed...

A photo-realist
 Chagall painted exactly what was up there
 in this case
 my grandmother
 on her second wedding day –

Vincenza
 the escapee
Vincenza
 the émigré
Vincenza
 the bride

so glad to be home
and en route to the piazza
to the puppet show, to Pulcinella
 Arlechino, Columbina
  to the fountain in the square of Casamassima

   where once so long ago her daughter's pet crow
    had followed a soap bubble too far into mystery
    too far into that frothy water world.

Today, however, he waits, preening
 and she takes him up
  and they waltz home together
   sharing chestnut songs.

While back across the sea
 in the cold little house in New York

   they comb out her auburn hair, plait it tight
   cross her hands over her heart
    try and ready her once more
     for a dark and narrow landing.

❧ Vincenza Not Landing ❧

Ninety years ago my grandmother floated towards this
world
    her ear pressed hard to the steel ship's floor
    the capricious waves beneath her cheek

Terrified to listen
    to eavesdrop on the abyss
    she cowered in the belly of her husband's chosen
whale
    daring neither movement nor sound of discontent,
instead
    evoking invisibility

Of course she was pregnant
    and hard to miss
    and a perfect tenant of the cattle hold
    which she shared with three hundred other restless
beings

so round-eyed and milky with such iron passivity
    she'd been easy to snatch from those azure grottos
    whose very stones had birthed her Mothers' mothers

and carry off to an Empire State, a right angle maze of
    amazing anglo files.

So seemingly easy my grandfather thought
    never noticing that his wife had avoided landing
    but kept floating backwards
    over the harbor
    like strains of an opera

too haunting too persistent…

❦ About the Author ❧

Patricia Catto was born in Auburn, New York, of Italian immigrants. She is the author of *Wife of Geronimo's Virile Old Age: Poems*, and many stories, articles, reviews and academic papers.

For twenty years, Patricia has taught at Kansas City Art Institute, offering a variety of courses exploring eco-psychological approaches to literature, and formal poetry writing centered on forms from the classical world to the contemporary marketplace. In the late 1990s she added the *raks sharki* dance element to her poetry classes and, in 2004 and 2006, traveled to India to study this form.

Patricia's courses in Folk Literature of the World are her signature and reveal a deep interest in the archetypal manifestations and soul motifs of our species. In 2001 Patricia began a series of dance-lectures entitled "Veil as Sacred Space," and has presented this workshop around the country.

She lives in Bisbee, Arizona, with her dogs, Habeebah, Ugoberto, Vito and Rhett Butler.

PATRICIA CATTO

34635173R00091

Made in the USA
Middletown, DE
29 August 2016